MEDITATIONS IN THE MOUNTAINS

Marion Rawson Vuilleumier

Abingdon Press
Nashville

MEDITATIONS IN THE MOUNTAINS

Copyright © 1983 by Marion Rawson Vuilleumier

All rights reserved.
No part of this book may be reproduced in any manner whatsoever without written permission of the publisher except brief quotations embodied in critical articles or reviews. For information address Abingdon Press, Nashville, Tennessee

Library of Congress Cataloging in Publication Data

VUILLEUMIER, MARION.
  Meditations in the mountains.
  1. Meditations. 2. Mountains—Religious aspects—Meditations. I. Title.
  BV4832.2.V78   1983   242   82-11523

ISBN 0-687-24260-6

I would like to express my appreciation to Marian Logan, who typed the manuscript for this book.

Scripture quotations noted RSV are from the Revised Standard Version of the Bible, copyrighted 1946, 1952, © 1971, 1973 by the Division of Christian Education of the National Council of Churches of Christ in the U.S.A., and are used by permission. All others are from the King James Version.

"Prayer at the Feet of Mountains" (p. 27) is from Grace Noll Crowell's *Light of the Years*, Copyright 1936 by Harper & Row, Publishers, Inc. "Pilgrimage" (pp. 79-80) is from Grace Noll Crowell's *Songs of Courage*, Copyright 1938 by Harper & Row, Publishers, Inc. "Summer Fields" (p. 102) is from Grace Noll Crowell's *Between Eternities*, Copyright 1944 by Harper & Row, Publishers. All three are used by permission of the publisher.

Thanks go to Lois Grant Palches for the use of her poem "God Is Wisdom" (p. 102) from *The Heart Is a Pendulum*.

"The Ways" (p. 82) is from *Gentlemen, the King!* by John Oxenham. Copyright 1928 by John Oxenham; copyright renewed 1956 by Erica Oxenham. Used by permission of Theo Oxenham and The Pilgrim Press.

MANUFACTURED BY THE PARTHENON PRESS AT
NASHVILLE, TENNESSEE, UNITED STATES OF AMERICA

To PIERRE DuPONT VUILLEUMIER

1908–1980

*To advantages of nature and
excellency of spirit, he added
an indefatigable industry, and
God gave a plentiful benediction.*

—Thomas Kepler

CONTENTS

Introduction..7
A Sacred Place..11
A Granite Core...13
Praise in Crystal...15
Glad Tidings..17
From Everlasting to Everlasting...................20
Flee to the Mountains..................................22
Thanks Giving...24
The Mountains Answer................................26
A Mysterious Fascination............................28
Doom in Twenty Years?..............................30
Like Snowflakes and Falling Rain................33
When Size Does Not Matter.......................35
Life amid Desolation...................................38
Encircling Arms...40
Many Trails, One Goal................................42
Centers of Renewal....................................45
A Mountain Mission....................................47
Living Well..49

The Signal	51
Change, A Fact of Life	53
Layers	55
One Step at a Time	57
A Free-flowing Spirit	60
On Being Present Where We Are	62
Barrier? Or Pathway?	64
An Alpine Visage	67
Sunrise Without and Within	69
Toward the Real	71
Disciplines	73
New Life out of Devastation	76
A Spiral of Prayer	78
The Hill Difficulty	80
Oneness	83
In, But Not of, The World	85
On Moving Mountains	87
Oxygen of the Spirit	89
Conquering an Everest	92
Symbols	94
Mists	96
The Intrinsic Value of Beauty	99
A Rainbow Vista	101
A Symbol of Peace	103
A Message Place	105
The Way	107
Silence	109
The Two Faces of Clouds	112
Beyond the Horizon	114
A Heavenly Voice	116
A Book of Hours	119
Receptivity	121
Down from the Mountain	123
He Depends on Us	125

INTRODUCTION

I came late to love mountains. What chance had I, when young, to know the majestic thrust of earth's highest elevations, with my early years spent among the low, rolling hills of Connecticut? Though pleasant and satisfying, views of those long ridges gave no hint of the awe-inspiring grandeur of their taller relatives, whose soaring summits bring a catch to the throat and a mist to the eye.

To be sure there were occasional trips to Grandmother's house in the midsection of Massachusetts, where Mount Watchuset stands. In my innocence I thought its rounded contour and height of 2,006 feet adequately portrayed a mountain, though there was a faint and elusive memory of higher peaks seen through morning mists on a family vacation in the Berkshires.

Thus as a teenager, I was unprepared for my first glimpse of tall mountains when our family journeyed one August to the White Mountains of New Hampshire. By then, though, I had studied the great elevations of the world in school and was eagerly anticipating my first view.

First came Mount Chocura, its sharp rocky escarpment more dramatic than anything I had seen before. Then my watchful eyes were rewarded with the majestic Presidentials—Mounts Madison, Adams, Jefferson, and Washington. Since Washington rose 6,288 feet above sea level, its height became increasingly more impressive as we drove closer. I remember sighing in satisfaction, thinking that these mountains were all I had hoped they would be.

Little did I realize that westerners would consider these mountains no more than foothills—that was a later discovery. For the present I was eminently satisfied that I knew mountains.

In a way that was true, for what I learned in that vacation week was the basis for later discoveries. I found that there are several ways to experience mountains, no matter what their size. First, one enjoys them from a distance, reveling in their importance among the natural phenomena of earth. Later, when one is closer, an overpowering sense of their strength and height is felt. It is almost as if one can absorb some of that ruggedness and strength by remaining near their bases. Finally, there is a special thrill reserved for the climber who toils to a mountaintop. The exhilaration of completing a challenging task is tempered with a sense of space and solitude that is experienced in no other place.

Some years later while climbing Mount Washington with a group of friends, I realized that I was "hooked" on mountains. For hours we had toiled upward and had finally reached the summit. Dropping breathlessly on its rocky top, I gazed out over a seemingly limitless display. Mountain after mountain rose in the distance. Peak after peak stretched to the horizon. It was almost stupefying to become aware of the breadth and scope of the earth. That sense of the vastness of God's world in contrast to the tenuousness of human life has never left me.

Then I married a minister and for eight happy years our

parsonage family lived in Laconia, New Hampshire, nestled among the mountains. I grew to love the terrain and the peaks in all their moods and seasons. Whether snowcapped, green-mantled, or scarlet-clad, they exuded serenity, peace, sanctuary.

When we had visitors, we invariably drove them to our favorite viewpoint on Gunstock Hill to show them the mountain vista seen over the expanse of Lake Winnipesaukee. If time permitted, we would borrow a friend's convertible and take our guests through the notches and passes of the White Mountains.

In later years we traveled to earth's other mountains, and my love and respect for them has grown. In our own country we have camped at the foot of the sharp-toothed Tetons of Wyoming, wandered among the alpine flowers in the high Rockies, and driven over snowy mountain passes on the Going-to-the-Sun Highway. One unforgettable morning when we were camped high on Mount Ranier, we rose before sunrise to see its rosy cone apparently hung in midair in the early morning light.

Other continents beckoned. On several occasions my husband and I traveled through or flew over the European Alps. We gazed in awe at the Matterhorn, Mount Blanc, and the Jungfrau. In Asia we flew alongside the Himalayas, looking out at Mount Everest, earth's highest peak, locked in its eternal snows.

As my love for mountains grew through the years, so also did my musings about their meaning in our lives. Some of those musings, I take pleasure in sharing with you.

Marion Vuilleumier
West Hyannisport,
Massachusetts

A Sacred Place

*And he brought them to the border of his sanctuary,
even to this mountain,
which his right hand had purchased.*
—Psalm 78:54

Throughout recorded time, like a recurring litany, there are references to the earth's high mountains as being sacred places—homes of gods. Apparently humans the world over have been sensitive to the strong spiritual forces that seem to be particularly evident in high elevations.

Just over a century ago the New England philosopher Henry David Thoreau noted this tendency. Commenting on the height, grandeur, and aloofness that give mountains an air of mystery, he added, "Simple races do not climb mountains—their tops are sacred and mysterious tracts never visited."

I thought of this not long ago while traveling in the Holy Land. Our party had just visited Jacob's Well in Samaria, and we were resting in the warm sun at its entrance. Directly above us loomed cone-shaped Mount Gerizim, its forested slopes thrusting dramatically upward from the valley floor. The Samaritans consider this limestone landmark their mountain of blessings. It sheltered their people in antiquity and was the location of their first temple, several centuries before the time of Christ. Today Mount Gerizim is as sacred to Samaritans as Jerusalem is to Jews and Mecca to Mohammedans. To these people who reside in its shadow, the mountain is a sanctuary, a place set apart, which brings them closer to God.

As I sat in the warm sun, my thoughts drifted to other mountains considered sacred. There was Sinai, revered by biblical ancients, as well as Olympus and Parnassus, reputedly the home of gods. In Asia, the Tibetan Mount Kailas is sacred to Hindus and Buddhists, while a mountain called Sun Chan is revered by the Chinese. In our own country, Wheeler Peak in New Mexico is a holy mountain to the Taos Indians; on it rests Blue Lake, for centuries a focal point of worship by these native Americans.

There *is* something about these high places that seems to elevate our moods. Anyone who has climbed a mountain knows that the soul of the climber does not remain untouched. The visitor to one of these immense masses is captivated by its stillness, its permanence, its majesty. The imagination is stimulated and the senses are heightened as the everyday world recedes and the inexorable force of the Creator emerges. It is not even necessary to be a climber to be aware of a mystical pull from beyond the self that occurs in the vicinity of mountains.

Remembering my own experiences of renewal on and near mountains, I gazed with respect at Mount Gerizim. The psalmist was correct, I thought; a mountain is like an enormous sanctuary where the heartbeat of the universe pulsates and where the power of the Creator is preeminent. These Samaritans, the native people everywhere, and the mountain lovers of today are right. A mountain is a sacred place that may bring us closer to God.

Creator of mountains, help us to see you in the majestic masses of earth's peaks. Enable us to sense your presence and renew our spirits as we rest among mountains or traverse their paths; in Jesus' name. Amen.

A Granite Core

*Lord, by thy favour thou hast made
my mountain to stand strong.*
—Psalm 30:7

Nowhere are we more conscious of the undergirding structure of the earth than on a high mountain. There we feel beneath our feet the bare bones of the land. These are the base of our globe, whether they underlie the restless sea or the fertile land.

The contrast between the softer trails of a mountain's lower slopes and the sharp bony face of its high peaks is sometimes quite marked. John Jerome, in his *On Mountains*, writes,

Suddenly, at about thirty-six hundred feet, we pop out into scrub fir forest, trees gone waist-high, miniaturizing on us. . . . The trail turns to solid granite, broken, tumbled, and irregular underfoot, but solid nevertheless, almost sidewalkish: the granite core of the mountain exposed, to be trod upon. It always surprises me. I know well enough in my head that mountains are all, always made of rock. But there's a permanent naivete down inside, the product perhaps of those years of digging holes in the back yard and daydreaming about reaching China. I still occasionally catch myself regarding mountains as piles of earth-soil, dirt, rather than solid rock with topsoil spread thinly over them as verdigris on a statue.

The psalmist David must have climbed to the tops of mountains and felt their rock-ribbed firmness under his feet, for when he offered a psalm and a song at the dedication of his house, praising God for many blessings, he included the strength of mountains. "Thou hast made my mountain to stand strong. . . . O Lord, my God, I will give thanks unto thee forever."

David, it seems, was impressed by the similarity between

the structure of mountains and that of humans. As the surface of mountains covers a firm rocky base, so also the outward personalities of men and women should envelope a firm undergirding—a faith that is similar to a mountain's granite core.

It is sobering to reflect upon this aspect of our lives. As we grow in mind and body, are we also growing in spirit? Under the surface, are we developing that solid faith that will carry us over the hard trails of life? Are we developing our own granite cores?

The noted author Catherine Marshall was faced with this question early in life. A serious illness would force her to remain in bed for a year and a half. The same day she received the discouraging diagnosis, she also received a gentle message from the Lord. In essence, it said to her, "Body is irretrievably tied to spirit: physical health will always be dependent upon spiritual health. For you, it is essential to begin every day with a quiet time with Me."

Out of that illness and the many quiet hours with the Lord has come a strong rocklike faith and a stream of inspirational classics, as well as guidance for the new publishing house, Chosen Books. In her recent book *My Personal Prayer Diary*, written with her husband, Leonard LeSourd, Catherine Marshall tells us: "In the years since, I have not always kept faith with this daily lifeline. But whenever I slip, I know what the trouble is and what to do about it."

Daily devotions and other spiritual exercises can assist us in developing a granite core of faith. Like a compass, this firm undergirding will help us stay on course under the normal circumstances of daily living. It will aso help us stand firm and unshaken when the storms of life rage around us. Our faith will enable us to join with David in psalms and songs, rejoicing that "thou has made my mountain to stand strong."

Heavenly Father, creator of both mountains and ourselves, help us to mature steadily through the years, so that when life's difficulties toss us to and fro, we can cut through the crust of our outward selves and cling to a firm and rocklike faith; in Jesus' name. Amen.

Praise in Crystal

*Great is the LORD and greatly to be praised
in the city of our God,
in the mountain of his holiness.*
—Psalm 48:1

Most of us are familiar with mountains in spring, summer, and fall, but not as many know mountains in winter. To be sure, snowcapped peaks are favorite subjects for photographers and painters—but their resulting artistry, like our own observations, are views from a distance. Mountains in winter are quite different when experienced close-by.

Skiers and mountaineers know a mountain's winter beauty firsthand. They have felt the pristine loveliness of expanses of unbroken snow and appreciated the fantastic snow sculptures created by the wind. They have breathed the invigorating pure mountain air and have gazed in awe at glaciers, those wondrous rivers of ice.

Switzerland is one of the best places to experience mountains in winter. There glistening peaks meet alpine-flowered meadows, and glaciers fill snow valleys. Laboring trains regularly chug up to the mountain passes that edge the snowfields, bringing shivering tourists to see the spectacular views.

One such visitor decades ago was Samuel Taylor Coleridge, who waxed lyrical in his "Hymn Before Sun-rise, in the Vale of Chamouni."

> Ye Ice-falls! ye that from the mountain's brow
> Adown enormous ravines slope amain—
> Torrents, methinks, that heard a mighty voice,
> And stopped at once amid their maddest plunge!
> Motionless torrents! silent cataracts!
> Who made you glorious as the Gates of Heaven
> Beneath the keen full moon? Who bade the sun
> Clothe you with rainbows? Who, with living flowers
> Of loveliest blue, spread garlands at your feet?—
> GOD! let the torrents, like a shout of nations,
> Answer! and let the ice-plains echo, GOD!
> GOD! sing ye meadow-streams with gladsome voice!
> Ye pine-groves, with your soft and soul-like sounds!
> And they too have a voice, yon piles of snow,
> And in their perilous fall shall thunder, GOD!

We can't all visit snowfields and glaciers, but we can, like Coleridge, see praise in crystal. Remember those fingers of ice that adorn the eaves of some of our homes in winter? When the rays of the sun sparkle through them prismlike, dancing crystals of light are reflected in our rooms. As the sun mounts higher and the rays grow warmer, drops of water are freed from their icy state, slide down the icicles, and drip to the ground. In their new freedom they seem to be exhibiting praise.

Can we humans do less than glaciers and icicles? "Great is the Lord and greatly to be praised," sang the psalmist. He seemed to advocate that we develop an attitude of continuous praise.

A friend confided recently that she had determined to do

just that after reading a little book entitled *Praise Works* by Merlin R. Carothers. She had made it a practice in recent weeks to begin her devotions with praise, instead of with petition.

"It is amazing," she said, "how a sensation of praise now wells up from my innermost being just as soon as I begin to pray. I am filled with a glow that carries over into the rest of my day."

Hymns and songs of praise are not new, of course, but sometimes I forget that an attitude of praise is the basis for prayer. When I do forget, perhaps a glimpse of ice crystals will remind me. Whether trapped in solid ice and praising through reflection, or mobile and praising with exuberant motion, they seem to magnify God. I can do no less and, like the psalmist, I will learn to praise God continuously throughout my days.

God of the natural world and of ours, help us to understand that praise is an integral part of prayer. Enable us to so discipline ourselves that magnifying you will become an instinctive process in our hearts; in Jesus' name. Amen.

Glad Tidings

Get you up to a high mountain,
O Zion, herald of good tidings.
—Isaiah 40:9 (RSV)

In the last century graceful clipper ships and sturdy whaling vessels ranged the seven seas, remaining away from home ports for months, sometimes even years. We can imagine with what eagerness their homecoming was awaited. The ingenious residents of Martha's Vineyard were determined not to wait a moment longer than necessary for news of their arrival. On that triangular-shaped island just off the Massachusetts coast, a complicated system of lights and flags was erected. From Sampson's Hill, Chappaquiddick, the island's highest point, this message system alerted the community to incoming ships.

Later, by means of hills and small mountains on the mainland, the exciting news of ship arrival was relayed farther. From Martha's Vineyard the glad tidings traveled over Cape Cod to Boston, Salem, and Newburyport in Massachusetts; to Portsmouth in New Hampshire; and finally to Portland, Maine. For decades the good news was sped along those earth mounds to waiting families and ship owners.

When the modern era of communications made this crude semaphore system obsolete, good news continued to be relayed from the mountaintops. First came the slender steel radio towers to carry the latest news from around the world. More recently these steel message carriers have been joined by giant saucers, which relay television pictures from space satellites. From the dawn of recorded history until this very day, glad tidings (as well as some not so glad) have come to us via mountaintops.

One wonders, though, if the significance of Isaiah's verse lies not only in its reference to the method of relaying news, but in its emphasis on the content of the message, for he particularly addresses bearers of *good* news. Is he indicating that we are to accentuate the positive and look particularly for glad tidings to relay? More specifically, is he urging us to speak out and let the world know when good things happen? When blessings come, are we to be sure to proclaim them?

Routine praise should be a habit of all of us, but here Isaiah seems to be talking about something more. When our hearts are almost bursting with praise because of special blessings, he urges us to share our good news with others.

With the modern communications available to us we do not need to go up on a mountain to spread our glad tidings. Letters can carry the news to relatives and friends. The telephone can spread joy instantly. Neighbors and church friends are folk to whom we can verbalize our happiness. A Miss America who has had a physical healing can use her appearances to witness for God. Those gifted with musical abilities can play or sing their good news. Those who write well can use books, magazines, newspapers, and the electronic media to pass along transforming experiences and words of heartfelt praise. Glad tidings are to be told to all, the Isaiah Scripture intimates, so that other lives may be touched.

God our Father, give us thankful hearts always, but especially when extra blessings come. Enable us to witness to our mountaintop experiences so that your name may be exalted and other lives transformed; in Jesus' name. Amen.

From Everlasting to Everlasting

*Lord, thou hast been our dwelling place in all generations.
Before the mountains were brought forth,
or ever thou hadst formed the earth and the world.*
—Psalm 90:1-2 (RSV)

It is not easy to comprehend the long march of generations and the great age of the world. Scientists tell us we live in only a tiny instant of recorded time, and the generations that stretch behind us represent but a fragment of the earth's existence. Yet this time is all we know. How are we to understand that the Creator has been our haven long before this moment?

A glimmer of understanding of God's time came to me while I was climbing Mount Washington with our youth fellowship group some years ago. The leader had majored in geology and now pointed out to our fascinated eyes the layers and strata in the raw earth beside the path. Along one trail a layer of sediment was tortuously twisted upward, mute evidence of folding—one way a mountain grows. Along another path we saw a fossilized fern caught in a rock, testimony that in another era that layer had been on a lower grassy plane. The Appalachian chain, of which this mountain is a part, was formed 350 to 400 million years ago. Since the earth is at least 4.6 billion years old, this mountain was relatively young, yet it had grown more slowly than at the proverbial snail's pace. Such ponderous movement is difficult to grasp, yet extremely enthralling.

This slow parade of the natural world reminds me of Margaret Drabble's character in *The Realms of Gold:*

[He] thought, not for the first time, that it would be his idea of heaven to sit on an observation platform somewhere and watch the earth change—watch mountains heave and fold, seas shrink, rivers wear down their valleys, continents drift and collide, forests dry into deserts and deserts burgeon into forests. The process, the constant flux, enthralled him.

An understanding of the process of mountain-making, the realization of the uncounted eons it has required, has given me a comprehension of endless time—God's time. It has helped me grasp what the psalmist meant when he said that God's care for us began "before the mountains were brought forth." This glimmer of comprehension, which came through an acquaintance with mountains, has been a great comfort, a solace, as I have wondered about the place of humans in such a vast and eternal universe.

My first thoughts of eternity, as a child, were frightening. The concept of time without end was so scary that I recall shutting off the thought with a snap, much like abruptly pulling down a shade. Only as I grew older and began to understand that God's time is not our time, that he was before and will be after our time, did I begin to pull up that mental shade. Gradually I cautiously peered again into that timeless scene, helped by passages such as our Scripture today.

Now I find great comfort in the magnificent parade of the physical world. If God has planned so carefully for the natural world, surely he must have a plan just as fine for humans, who were created in his own image. It is easier now to trust him and raise my mental shade even higher. Suddenly I realize that the world beyond this is no longer frightening. I can look forward into eternity with confidence. I am no longer terrified by the words "from everlasting to everlasting."

Father of earth's eons as well as of human generations, help us to understand, through knowing the physical world, the meaning of your love and care in the spiritual world. Enable us to grow in trust, so that we can face both the near future and the far future in confidence and serenity, knowing you are always with us; in Jesus name. Amen.

Flee to the Mountains

*In the Lord put I my trust:
how say ye to my soul,
Flee as a bird to your mountain?*
—Psalm 11:1

In the gray dawn, a scientist stood on the crest of a mountain in the Allegheny range of West Virginia. On one side of the rocky pinnacle, the waters drained east to the Atlantic Ocean. On the other, the streams and rivers flowed westward toward the Mississippi. Though the view over the misty mountaintops was breathtaking, the scientist paid no attention, for he was engrossed in the banding of birds.

He had difficulty keeping abreast of the stream of birds being brought to him by the enthusiasts of the bird club from Wheeling. The members were netting those tiny feathered creatures in great numbers, interrupting the southern migration momentarily so that they could be counted in the annual bird census.

Though pushed to the limit, the scientist paused momentarily to admire a ruby-crowned Kinglet and a black-throated Blue Warbler held captive in his gentle fingers. Hardly longer than his forefinger, these birds were on their way from northern mountains in the United States and Canada to the southern shores of the Atlantic Ocean. Some of the frail, feathered folk would journey ten thousand miles in their annual migration. Quickly the scientist attached leg bands as light as one of their feathers, and these two amazing creatures were off in the air again.

Heading south to the shores of the Caribbean and even South America, the birds would winter in warm climes, then unerringly retrace their steps to the mountain vastnesses. Along the way these little beings would probably rest in the same trees they had visited on earlier trips. Upon their return some would seek out the same location, even the very branches where they had raised earlier broods. Always they would persist until they reached their mountain homes.

Sometimes I feel a great affinity for my friends the birds, who fly so unerringly to their mountain habitations in spite of the vagaries of the weather or the interference of bird-banding humans. The tiny winged beings seem to know that beyond these present distractions lies a place of refuge.

I have distractions, too. There are deadlines to be met, household tasks to be completed, and duties to be performed with family and friends. If these come along in orderly procession, they are pleasures. If they all occur at the same time, it is easy to become distraught. It is then that I think of the psalmist's remark, "Flee as a bird to your mountain."

I cannot always literally escape to the mountains, for the nearest are more than one hundred fifty miles distant. However, having been there, I can recreate their quietness and strength within my heart. I can find a quiet corner in my home, shut my eyes, and recall the sense of peace and serenity found among the mountains. I can see once again the mountain streams dashing joyously downward over granite rocks. I can smell the tall pines in the thick forest. I can hear the twittering of birds in the branches and recall the vastness of the view from the crest.

From some source I cannot define but which never fails, a sense of peace and quiet descends, and I am thankful that I too, like my feathered friends, can flee to the mountains.

Our gracious Father who cares for both tiny birds and larger humans, enable us to remember mountain sanctuaries and reach out for the renewal they bring; in Jesus' name. Amen.

Thanks Giving

*As fire consumes the forest,
as the flame sets the mountains ablaze.*
—Psalm 83:14 (RSV)

At no time are the hills and mountains more glorious than in autumn when they are robed in scarlet and gold; when the sunlight, like a magic wand, turns them into shimmering splendor finer than the most precious jewels. In the places of earth where the seasons change, this miracle takes place in autumn.

One such fall day, we drove in an open car through the White Mountains of New Hampshire. Far from white now, the mountains revealed ever more breathtaking vistas around each bend in the road. The brilliant colors of the oaks and maples blended with the greens of the pines and cedars to create a vibrant tapestry—almost like a moving fire.

I thought of the psalmist who spoke of a flame that set a mountain ablaze. He may have been describing a burning forest fire, but I like to think it was a scene similar to this.

It is no coincidence, I thought, that autumn is the time of Thanksgiving. Humans join nature in giving thanks and praise. That celebration is held in November and is a national holiday in the United States. But long before the Christian era, times of rejoicing and thanks-giving to the God of all were held at the end of each growing season. Now the hills again join with humans in their age-old routine.

As the mountainside gave thanks in color, I wondered if we humans remember to give thanks at times other than this special season. Nature must follow a prescribed cycle, but we are free to rejoice and give thanks at any time.

I recalled the story of Mike, a young man who worked at a small art colony in Hawaii. It was in the 1930s amid a severe depression. A writer at the colony, who was jobless, noticed that Mike was consistently cheerful, though he did not have a great deal of this world's goods.

"What good fairy waved her wand over you and provided all your needs?" he asked. For answer, Mike took the writer to his room and pointed to a string of letters over the bed: L I D G T T F T A T I M.

"What are they?" joked the writer. "Open sesame to a treasure cave?"

"They are for me," Mike answered, and he explained that in a time of discouragement a teacher had introduced him to the power of praise and thankfulness. "The letters stand for the words LORD, I DO GIVE THOUGHTFUL THANKS FOR THE ABUNDANCE THAT IS MINE. I say them daily in gratitude and thanksgiving, and the Lord has brought good things my way."

We drove on through the glorious day, returning at dusk,

almost wordless after the beauty we had seen. If the hills and vales can give thanks so profoundly, we can too, I thought, determined to make Mike's words part of my daily prayers.

Lord, may we always remember to stress the blessings we have received, rather than the troubles we face. Help us to be positive instead of negative, giving thanks in all things; in Jesus' name. Amen.

The Mountains Answer

*I cry aloud to the Lord,
and he answers me from his holy hill.*
—Psalm 3:4 (RSV)

Occasionally the frets and cares of life seem to crush us. Like a heavy pack on our back, they drain our energy, slow our movements, and hold us back from projects that cry for completion.

Perhaps our child anguishes between the difficult right and the easy wrong. Maybe there is a forked road before us and we know not which path to take. Perhaps the pile of unanswered letters on our desk is overwhelming. It might be the illness of a loved one that causes a dark cloud to descend upon us when we wake in the morning and hover over us through the day, as we go forward like an automaton.

Then it is good to slip away from the daily routine and the

incessant demands of our schedule, to a place set apart. Often that place of refuge is in the mountains.

I recall escaping from hectic days some years ago by traveling northward to Campton, New Hampshire, and a high plateau with a breathtaking view of the Presidential peaks—Washington, Adams, Jefferson, and Madison. Here on the fertile plain of an ancient farm I relaxed and drank in that spectacular vista. Words were unnecessary as my companions and I watched the vivid blues of the sky change to deep purple and the violet shadows gather on the slopes. As the mists collected in the valleys, the mountains layered, then gradually faded in the gathering twilight, I recalled a poem by Grace Noll Crowell, "Prayer at the Feet of the Mountains."

> Maker of mountains—
> Creator of their beauty and their might,
> I lift my small and human heart to Thee.
> Fill it, I pray, with something of their might,
> Their steadfastness, their high serenity;
> Sweep it with canyon winds, and wash it clean
> With clear cold water from the eternal snow.
> Let these bright torrents purge it, let all mean
> Desires and passions leave it—let me go
> Back to the lowlands, back to crowded days,
> Poised and sustained, and ready for my part.
> Let me go back, schooled in the mountains' ways,
> Bearing their old vast secrets in my heart.

In a manner mysterious to me, the mountains had been a conduit for a message from the Creator. I had received an answer although I had not knowingly asked a question. I had fled from the lowland, realizing only I needed the high serenity of the mountains. Now I was returning with a lighter heart.

Our Father God, thank you for transcendent moments when eternal truths and creative power flow to us from you. Help us to recall these moments when hectic days pressure us; in Jesus' name. Amen.

A Mysterious Fascination

I will lift up my eyes to the hills.
—Psalm 121:1 (RSV)

What is the mysterious fascination that hills and mountains have for us? No matter how long I gaze at them, it is never enough. I turn away with regret and long to return again. Others must feel so, too, for at every spot on this earth where mountains thrust upward, there are resorts that feature mountain views, highway lookout spots that reveal spectacular sights, and paintings of mountains available to stimulate inspiring memories.

I wonder if this mysterious pull is the Creator's call to each individual to climb higher on the road of life, to regain a forgotten ideal, or to build more noble aspirations. Could it be that the One behind this natural phenomenon is urging us to absorb the strength and steadfastness of these giants?

Apparently that is what Nathaniel Hawthorne thought when he wrote his epic story "The Great Stone Face." He was inspired by New Hampshire's famous tourist attraction, the Old Man of the Mountain, in Franconia. According to Fredrika Burrows, writing in the June 1974 *New Hampshire Profiles,* this granite rock jumble on Cannon (or Profile) Mountain was created by the glacier many centuries ago.

When viewed from the lakeshore below, the series of ledges and boulders appear to outline the rugged profile of a man's face. Though Indians knew it in prehistory, the white man's discovery dates to 1805, when it immediately became "the most widely viewed and most famous attraction in the White Mountains."

Hawthorne, immensely impressed by this Titan "with its massive forehead; long nose; the parted lips, mute but capable of thunder accents throughout the valley," composed a tale of a boy called Ernest who had been born under the shadow of the Great Stone Face. The child often gazed upward, wishing the great visage could speak. "It looks so kindly and pleasant. Should I ever see a man like that I would dearly love him."

"An old prophesy has it," responded his mother, "that some time we will see a man with a face like that."

She then recounted a legend "murmured by the streams and whispered by the trees first to the Indians and then to the palefaces . . . that sometime a child would be born who would become the greatest man of his times, and whose face in maturity would exactly resemble the Great Stone Face."

Through the years, Ernest waited for the prophesy to be fulfilled, all the while gazing in veneration at the face. Often as he looked upward when his day's labor was finished, he felt recognized and encouraged in return. From time to time, famous men born in the valley came home to receive the approbation of the inhabitants—a financier, a general, a politician—but Ernest looked at each one in vain for the likeness.

Finally, when Ernest was an old man, a hometown poet returned to the valley. Ernest, now venerated for his wisdom and consulted by the learned of the land, addressed the townspeople from a natural outdoor pulpit. As the poet watched and listened, the setting sun illumined the Great Stone Face.

Glancing from that visage to Ernest, the poet exclaimed, "Behold, the likeness of the Great Stone Face is found at last in Ernest." The people declared this to be true, but Ernest modestly escorted the visiting poet to his cottage, "hoping a wiser and better man would appear bearing the likeness."

"I will lift up my eyes to the hills," sang the psalmist long ago. I believe that he was intent on absorbing their nature.

Our Father who has given us a deep appreciation for hills and mountains, help us to absorb their characteristics. May these towering magnets influence us to follow in their ways and enlarge our souls; in Jesus' name. Amen.

Doom in Twenty Years?

*O many-peaked mountain,
mountain of Bashan.
—Psalm 68:15b (RSV)*

Some years ago our family vacationed in the Rockies, that magnificent chain of mountains that rises in the American West. One memorable day we drove the fifty-mile Going-to-the-Sun Highway in Glacier National Park, Montana. The spectacular drive winds around peaks that thrust upward nine and ten thousand feet. There are waterfalls, glaciers, rapids, and occasionally a blue gem of a lake. There was a harsh beauty about these sharp escarpments silhouetted against the azure sky, for these are younger mountains, not yet scourged to a rounded gentleness by the elements as are the eastern Appalachians. Every turn brought views of new summits, some snow-covered even though it was July. I felt as the psalmist did when he exclaimed over the many-peaked mountain of Bashan.

When we stopped for lunch at an overlook well off the highway, we seemed isolated from all the world. Gradually we stopped chattering as the mountains cast their spell. Nature in one of its finest garbs seemed overpowering. The experience was the more forceful because there was not a soul in sight. Even the faint chugging of a motor in the distance failed to break the feeling of aloneness.

Years later I remembered that feeling as I traveled through India, one of the world's most populated countries. It required an entire day to bus from New Delhi to Sat Tal, a retreat center of the United Christian Ashrams in the foothills of the Himalayas, and I was struck by the number of people at every turn. When we left the city early that morning, we had passed people sleeping on sidewalks and roadsides. As the bus laboriously ground its way across the countryside, there were people working in the fields, tending water buffalo, working the simple pumps, and washing clothes by the streams.

In the villages we were surrounded by crowds who stared as if memorizing every detail of our faces and dress. At times it was unnerving and we made progress by inches. Throughout the entire day, there was not one moment when humans were absent from the landscape.

On the return trip in a station wagon driven by a local missionary, we picnicked by a stream. I was surprised to see our hostess leave the paper plates and remainder of our lunch on the grassy bank.

"No trash pickup needed here," she laughed. "The

moment we leave, every scrap will be snatched by the villagers. Nothing is wasted in India."

I reflected on this experience during the rest of the trip. Those of us who live in less-crowded sections of the world find it hard to understand the meaning of overpopulation. Unless we actually see the overcrowding, it is easy to ignore the problem. What a contrast to the aloneness I had felt in Montana!

Early in 1981, representatives of sixty organizations met in Washington, D.C., for a Leadership Conference on Population, Resources, and the Environment. Conferees there warned that the drain of an accelerating population on planetary reserves will be severe—and will become frightening by the time today's toddler reaches the age of twenty. After the conference, columnist Richard L. Strout remarked, "The earnest delegates want to get the nation's attention. Will anybody listen? Who knows?"

Former President Jimmy Carter spoke of the problem in his farewell address: "There are real and growing dangers to our simple and most precious possessions: the air we breathe, the water we drink, and the land which sustains us. . . . If we do not act now, the world of A.D. 2000 will be much less able to sustain life than it is now."

I love mountain vistas and the sense of closeness to the Creator that these inspire, but I hope such experiences will not lull me into a false sense of security as the earth's billions increase.

Our Heavenly Father who created both peaks and people, help us to understand that both need to be protected on this globe. Give us the wisdom and the will to find creative solutions to this dilemma; in Jesus' name. Amen.

Like Snowflakes and Falling Rain

*In his hand are the depths of the earth;
the heights of the mountains are his also.*
—Psalm 95:4 (RSV)

I shall never forget the thrill I felt when I first stood on the Continental Divide, watershed of the continent. We had followed the winding Trail Ridge Road through Rocky Mountain National Park in Colorado one summer day. The scenic beauty was almost overwhelming as we drove through Arctic tundra, below and above the timberline. The variety of natural formations included lofty peaks, rock ridges, needle-sharp crags, sheer cliffs. A covering of snow at the highest elevations added drama to the peaks silhouetted against a cobalt sky.

Finally at the 10,759-foot Miller Pass, we stopped at a simple sign that read Continental Divide. We stepped out of the car, awed to realize that we were standing on the backbone of North America. Toward the west, all waters flowed toward the Pacific Ocean. On the east, each rivulet joined others, finally reaching the Gulf of Mexico, or the Atlantic or Arctic oceans. Snow and rain that fell on the continent's crown would someday find its way into the depths of the sea.

The words of the psalmist were appropriate. "In his hand are the depths of the earth: the heights of the mountains are his also." In one great cycle of climate, God has revealed his dominance over the earth from the depths to the heights.

But the word *divide* seemed to have a deeper significance. Here before me were two paths to follow, an eastern or a western route, depending upon where each snowflake or raindrop fell. They had no choice. Their route was dictated entirely by chance.

Sometimes humans are in the same situation. Ideally, we have a choice of divergent paths. There are times, though, when we seemed to be locked into one path by circumstances beyond our control.

Our families, for example, are ours for better or for worse. We do not choose to abandon them when times are hard. Some folks have regretfully relinquished a career in order to carry on a family business. Others, because of circumstances, have remained on paths they would not otherwise have chosen. Like the snowflakes or raindrops, they were locked into a position, with no way out. How should we respond to these watersheds, or Continental Divides, in our lives?

This unanswered question hung in the recesses of my mind for years, until I came across a personal experience in *The Intercessors* newsletter. Catherine Marshall told of her friend Marge, who was desolated when her husband's illness was diagnosed as Parkinson's Disease. The family gathered, anointed him, and prayed for healing. But Marge wondered, "Until such time as our family sees this prayer answered, how can I keep enough peace of mind not to let worry and fear impede or stop my daily work?"

Later Marge stepped aboard a plane, and as she buckled herself into her seat she noticed a strange phenomenon. On one side of the plane a sunset suffused the entire sky with glorious color. But through the window on the other side, Marge could see only the dark, threatening clouds. There was no indication of the beautiful sunset. As the plane began to lift into the sky, Marge felt she heard a gentle voice speaking to her.

You have noticed the windows. . . . For awhile now your life will contain some happy, beautiful times, but also some dark shadows. Here's a lesson I want to teach you to save you much heartache and allow you to abide in Me with continual peace and joy. . . . You see, it doesn't matter which window you look through, this plane is still going to Cleveland.

So it is in your life. You can dwell on the gloomy picture. Or you can focus on the bright things of your life and leave the dark, ominous situations to Me. I alone can handle the dark ones anyway. And the final destination is not influenced by what you see and hear along the way.

Dear Father who is as close to us as to the snowflakes and the raindrops, help us to accept what we cannot change and to glorify our daily moments. Give us strength to look at the bright side as we proceed on the necessary pathway to our eternal home; in Jesus name. Amen.

When Size Does Not Matter

*The pastures of the wilderness drip,
the hills gird themselves with joy.*
—Psalm 65:12 (RSV)

I was on a high mountain meadow in the Rockies when I realized that in God's eyes, size does not matter. We had driven over a series of mountain passes that August day in Colorado. Our car had carefully hugged a gray ribbon of road that wound around tall peaks and edged deep ravines. Patches of snow covered the ground in some places, for even in summer this trail is well above the timberline. At one stop, the children had a snowball fight.

We stopped for lunch on a mountain meadow and reached for sweaters in the invigorating air. The treeless expanse of tundra was broken only by boulders, we thought, until we looked downward. Here in this inhospitable expanse we saw tiny mountain blossoms nestled upon the ground. There were dainty lavender daisies, yellow buttercups, and pink dwarf clover. They were so small we had to kneel to appreciate this miniature garden of alpine flowers.

Later I read ecologist Beatrice Willard's comments about these mountain flowers in the book *America's Magnificent Mountains*. This teacher at the Aspen Center for Environmental Studies noted, "You have to lie flat to see half the species. . . . Small size is an advantage in the Arctic climate of the tundra. Plants with small leaves, short stems, and few flowers more easily complete their growth in the brief, often interrupted summer. Growing close to the ground reduces exposure to the wind and increases retention of solar heat."

I have often wondered if the psalmist, who so long ago noted the pastures and hills that girded themselves with joy, had climbed Israel's snow-topped Mount Hermon. Had he seen tiny alpine flowers blossoming in its high places? Had he rejoiced at their efforts to praise the Creator by fulfilling their mission in a difficult area?

I was reminded of those tiny flowers when I read an account of a remarkable conference, in an April 1981 issue of the *Christian Science Monitor*. Cynthia Parsons reported on the initial gathering in Caracas, Venezuela, of philanthropists, entrepreneurs, heads of foundations, and business leaders. They came from Europe and the two Americas to discuss the global problems of pollution, overpopulation, and food shortage. They also shared ideas about possible answers—teaching illiterates, establishing health centers, arranging low-interest loans for small businesses, encouraging voluntary contributions from the public.

Though the delegates heard addresses by David Rockefeller, Adlai Stevenson, III, and government officials who were agents for dispensing large amounts of foreign aid, I was struck by the recurring note of amazing success in smaller efforts—one individual helping another, the one-to-one, or heart-to-heart, approach.

Venezuela had created a $23-package of five workbooks and a recorder, in a nationwide literacy campaign. With this packet, one person teaches five others to read. Then each of the five, armed with a packet, teaches five more people.

In Haiti there is a new foundation which provides low-interest loans to small businesses. In Brazil a new program prepares village children for school while their mothers are at work.

Parsons reported, "The proverb 'Give a man a fish and you satisfy his hunger once; teach him to fish and you remove his hunger' could be called the keynote of this conference."

Could miniature blossoms in alpine meadows be reminding us that earth-threatening problems can sometimes be solved by a myriad of small efforts? Are these flowers sending the message that what the world needs is not a moaning and groaning over our ineffectiveness, but rather a simple helping hand from one soul to another—multiplied many times?

God of the small as well as of the large, teach us to appreciate the miniature in life—whether plants that bloom in difficult terrain or human efforts that seem miniscule in the light of world problems. Give to each of us the desire and the will to stretch forth our hands and hearts in helpfulness and love; in Jesus' name. Amen.

Life amid Desolation

*Then the earth reeled and rocked;
the foundations also of the mountains trembled.*
—Psalm 18:7 (RSV)

We were standing on the rim of the volcanic crater of Haleakala (House of the Sun) on the island of Maui in Hawaii. When measured from the ocean floor to the summit, it is the tallest volcano on earth. Its eruptions are long past, and it is safe to visit this mountain, which is now a national park.

Everywhere we looked, the results of ancient upheavals could be seen. The jumble of rocks, the scattered cinder cones, the black lava flows were evidences of the cataclysms that had taken place from prehistory to 1790. As the psalmist said, the earth had reeled and rocked. I felt a sense of desolation.

Earlier that morning we had driven up a winding road around frightening switchbacks to the visitors center, then climbed a rocky path to the summit. Now I stood awed by the expanse of the inner cone, so large it could hold the entire island of Manhattan. I marveled at the energy that had propelled this mass of rock and lava upward from the ocean floor. I saw no trees, shrubs, or any sign of life. The sense of desolation persisted.

Then I gasped. There was a slender-stemmed pale green plant growing out of a rocky crevice.

"It's a silversword, one of the world's endangered species," commented the guide who had joined us. "This is the only place in the world they grow. You can see a small patch of them in an enclosure as you climb down the crater's edge."

Later I stood transfixed at the ethereal beauty of the silverswords. The otherworldly effect was heightened by the sun's rays as they shone through the gray mist, for by now it was close to noon and the summit of Haleakala was collecting its usual clouds. The plants stood proud and tall, reaching toward heaven. How they could receive nourishment from such rocky terrain was a mystery to me. It was extraordinary to find life among such desolation.

As I absorbed this will to live, even among the rubble, I thought of Helen Keller, who triumphed over almost insurmountable handicaps. At the age of nineteen months, she had contracted a fever that left her blind and deaf. Unable to communicate, for nearly six years she was wild and unruly, with no knowledge of the world. "I was like an unconscious clod of earth," she later observed.

Then through the suggestion of Alexander Graham Bell, Helen's parents contacted Perkins School for the Blind and secured twenty-year-old Annie Sullivan to be Helen's teacher. The thrilling story of Miss Sullivan's patient work and the eventual breakthrough is familiar to the world through William Gibson's play *The Miracle Worker.*

Despite the overwhelming odds, Helen learned to speak, write, and use the typewriter. She was graduated cum laude from Radcliffe College in 1904 and authored eleven books. She lectured widely on behalf of the blind and deaf, encouraging other handicapped people to develop their full potential.

In *My Religion,* she tells her life story and her spiritual odyssey. "Truly I have looked into the heart of darkness, and refused to yield to its paralyzing influence. In spirit I am one of those who walk in the morning."

Silverswords and the late Helen Keller—both reveal life amid desolation. Surely, I thought, God is telling us that there is no place on earth where life is impossible, no corner of the human heart where the flame of eternity cannot be felt.

Our Father God who is in the darkness as well as in the light, in rocky terrain as well as in green meadows, help us to remember that you are in and among all things. Guide us in encouraging others and in keeping our own spirits aflame when life's pathway traverses trails of desolation; in Jesus' name. Amen.

Encircling Arms

*As the mountains are round about Jerusalem,
so the Lord is round about his people,
from this time forth and for evermore.*
—Psalm 125:2 (RSV)

Mountains have always seemed friendly and comforting to me. Therefore it was a great surprise to find that, to some people, they are frightening.

One summer day our family picnicked on the shore of a lake at the foot of Cannon Mountain. We were in Franconia Notch, which is so closely surrounded by steep mountains that we felt we could almost reach out and touch them. As we admired the view, an out-of-state car drew up and a couple joined us at the lakeside.

"Isn't this magnificent?" exclaimed my husband, who was readying his camera for a picture.

"I find it quite frightening," shivered the woman, her face somber. "I'm used to the Great Plains, where nothing is in sight for miles."

She was from Kansas, I noted from their license plate.

She shivered again. "I feel closed in, caught in a web."

I mused often about that incident, wondering why there

should be two such differing reactions to high mountains. But it was not until many years later when I was in a plane descending to the Jerusalem airport that I was struck by a glimmer of understanding.

The jet circled lower and lower, giving a clear view of the ancient city that is so sacred to Christians, Jews, and Moslems. It is clearly ringed with mountains, which encircle the city almost as though they are safeguarding it from an unfriendly world.

Maybe, I thought, one's reaction to mountains is conditioned by one's point of view. If we only look upward at them, we see just their sharp, forbidding escarpments, their rock outcroppings that could crush us if they fell. But if we climb them or fly over them, we see how they protect the surrounding plains. We then relax, as their fearsomeness melts away. It is all in the point of view.

Marjorie Holmes, author of many inspirational columns and books, wrote about point of view in the September 1979 *Guideposts*. "The only thing I don't like about this house," she told her husband and the real estate agent, "is the kitchen windows. I'm so short and they are so high."

"Maybe we can see about lowering them," her husband responded, so they bought the house. But they were too busy with other projects to do anything about the windows. Though she fretted at first, she soon realized that she had gradually absorbed a wonderful new perspective. Instead of gazing across the yard or into a neighbor's window, she was viewing sunrises in the morning and the last lingering color of the evening sky. She watched birds as they built nests and saw clouds changing shape as they drifted by. While the usual mundane activities were going on outside, she had grown intimate with treetops and sky. It was the same high window, but her point of view had changed.

Musing further, I decided that this is true of problems in our lives. Sometimes they loom as terrifying as high mountains. But if we examine them from all sides, we may find they are not so frightening and that the psalmist's words are true. As the mountains are round about Jerusalem, so the Lord is near his people with encircling arms. I could only hope that a closer acquaintance with mountains has brought this same comfort to my acquaintance from Kansas.

Our heavenly Father who is ever ready to provide comfort in terrifying situations, help us to face these squarely, whether they be nature's mountains or mountains of problems. Enable us to live so close to you that we can feel your encircling arms guiding and protecting us; in Jesus' name. Amen.

Many Trails, One Goal

*Come, let us go up to the mountain of the Lord,
to the house of the God of Jacob.*
—Micah 4:2 (RSV)

How many trails there are that lead up a mountain! In searching for the summit, climbers try first one then another until they finally realize their goal.

The Matterhorn in Switzerland, a mountain of many trails, was an extreme challenge for many years. It is not

Switzerland's tallest, yet it rises vertically in steep, sharp cliffs. It pierces the sky like a sword and is as difficult to climb. In spite of many attempts no one had reached the summit until 1865, almost one hundred years after its higher neighbor, Mount Blanc, was conquered.

In the process of achieving the Matterhorn's crown, several attack routes were tried. All those from the southwest ridge failed. Many more attempts from the northwest ridge also failed.

Finally the English artist and avid mountaineer Edward Whymper determined to reach the top. According to Lowell Thomas in *A Book of High Mountains,* Whymper made a half-dozen attempts via both the southwest and the northeast ridges. Finally he triumphed by climbing the east face and the northeast ridge. He and his party of seven raised a makeshift flag on the top, which told watchers below in Zermatt that the majestic mountain finally had been tamed. The triumph was dimmed, however, by the tragic loss of four of the party on the descent.

On lower, more gradual mountains, like Mount Washington in New Hampshire, there are many trails to choose from. Though they vary in length, grade, markings, and difficulty, the goal is always the same—to reach the top.

Is this not somewhat like the human outreach toward God? The ways to look for him are infinite—as varied as the snowflakes—because each one of us is unique. Yet the goal is singular and universal.

Quaker Barry Morley confirms this in the July 1, 1981, *Friends Journal.* "In a meeting for worship I have heard the Way described as a quest of a mountain. Many paths start from many places, but there is only one place to arrive." He calls this Way "the path over which we walk hand in hand with the Light toward the throne."

Morley recommends visualization as an aid:

Slow down your conscious, outward-looking, problem-solving mind and move toward the stillness of your inward-reaching mind, the quiet place you touch when meeting for worship works just right or when you have not quite fallen asleep. . . . See yourself walking hand-in-hand with Light toward the place beyond time where the stars sing together.

I remember anguishing in earlier years because I could not point to an experience in my pilgrimage that was like any I had read about. There had been no Damascus Road, no sudden conversion. Yet, on reflection, why should there be, since I was raised in a Christian home and grew gradually into the faith? Yet I continued to wonder if I was on the true Way.

Consistent reading of spiritual biographies and of that exceedingly helpful little magazine *Guideposts* revealed how many are the ways to God. I finally relaxed, waiting in faith. Then one morning in the midst of a Quaker meeting, I experienced a living presence. I realized that my way is different, but no less real than that of another. We are called only to be faithful and to follow the way that opens to us. Our path will eventually lead to our spiritual summit—contact with the Eternal.

Our Father, guide us on the many pathways that lead to you, be close to each of us as we follow the pathway designed for us. Inspire and strengthen us as we climb the Lord's mountain toward our eternal home; in Jesus' name. Amen.

Centers of Renewal

*Come ye, and let us go up
to the mountain of the LORD.*
—Isaiah 2:3

I shall never forget my first view of the Cascade Range that dominates the Pacific Northwest. Our family was traveling west toward Seattle, Washington, to visit friends, when suddenly a row of serrated peaks appeared on the horizon. Their jagged crests, born of volcanic fire and shaped by glacial ice, were unlike any others I had seen. One giant was Mount Saint Helens, which gave no hint of the eruption to come in the spring of 1980.

As we neared, we could see snow on the highest peaks, though it was midsummer. I was to learn later that the Cascades hold more glacial ice than all the mountains in the United States combined, except those in Alaska. According to *America's Magnificent Mountains,* national parks protect 1.2 million acres of this spectacular terrain while the National Forest Service administers the remaining 14 million acres. As I looked at that remote perpendicular outline, the thought of inhabitants in the inhospitable terrain was far from my mind.

But I discovered that the Cascades are populated, though sparsely in the higher sections. I also found that one person had heeded the call of the Scripture to "go up to the mountain of Jehovah" and had established a religious community close to this Glacier Peak wilderness.

Holden, once a copper mining center, had become a ghost town in 1957 when the mines closed. A farsighted layman had persuaded the mining company to give the site to a nonprofit Lutheran corporation in 1960. Volunteers donated time and money to renovate the village which now serves as a year-round retreat. Guests, numbering close to four hundred each summer, listen to lectures, participate in craft classes, discuss religious and social issues, as well as fish and hike in the Cascades.

Author H. Robert Morrison on a recent visit was struck by the sense of community he discovered. Werner Jansse, the business manager, told him, "People find here an atmosphere that offers time for individual meditation and development and the support of a concerned group of Christians."

I thought of other retreat centers I had known, from Geneva Point in New Hampshire to Forest Home, California. It was not by chance, I thought, that these places of rest and renewal were set amid mountains. There is something about the isolation that permits us to rearrange our priorities. In the magnificent natural world, our attention becomes less centered on self. We are more free to experience the power described by Merlin in Mary Stewart's *Last Enchantment:* "Some power there is that draws men's eyes and hearts up and outward, beyond the heavy clay that fastens them to earth."

I recalled another quote about power, written by Walter Lanyon in *Union Life* magazine. "Not until man comes to identify himself intimately with God, can he feel the Unconditional Power moving within and without him."

In mountains like the Cascades, with their expansiveness and magnificence, it is easier to find this creative power. Blessings on the countless people who have heeded Isaiah's call to go up to the mountain and have established these centers of renewal.

Father God, creator of mountains in all their awesomeness, help us to open our finite hearts to you. Fill us with your love and power, that these may overflow into the lives of those around us; in Jesus' name. Amen.

A Mountain Mission

*How beautiful upon the mountains
are the feet of him that bringeth good tidings.*
—Isaiah 52:7

When I think of missionaries, I always place them against a hot, humid background—India, Africa, the islands. For some strange reason I have never thought of them in colder climes amidst mountain snows. Yet one of the earliest missionaries in Europe was Bernard, who established a hospice in a mountain pass in the year 962.

Born in Menthon, France, in 923, Bernard took holy orders and eventually became Archdeacon of Aosta. When he was requested to clear a high pass of brigands and thieves, Bernard found a need for a permanent place of refuge. Thus in this cleft between Italy and Switzerland, he began an outreach to pilgrims and other travelers in one of the highest parts of the world. Bernard and his monks fed and lodged wayfarers, entertained pilgrims on the way to Rome, cared for the sick, and made frequent trips on each side of the pass to rescue those lost in deep snow.

Through the centuries, this mission continued. To assist in their efforts, the monks bred intelligent, loyal Alpine sheep dogs to strong, courageous bulldogs. The result was the Saint Bernard of today. The work of the monks and dogs became legend. The Saint Bernards plodded ahead, searching the drifts for the fallen, followed by the monks on skis. When the lost were found, a flask of brandy on the dog's collar revived the sick, and together, dogs and men brought travelers to safety.

How beautiful upon the mountains are the feet of those (whether four- or two-footed) who bring glad tidings!

I have often thought with gratitude of the dedication shown by missionaries. Leaving loved ones and a prescribed, protected life, they venture into the unknown to aid the needy of body and soul. Not counting the cost, they press forward, following the leading of the Spirit, to places where their talents can best be used. I remind myself to hold present-day mission folk regularly in prayer, for they need our material and prayer support as much as we need to have them representing us in the front lines.

In the South Congregational Church in Centerville, Massachusetts, there is a prayer group where, each week, faithful members remember missionaries in prayer, and birthday cards are mailed monthly to the far reaches of the globe. The members are aided by a *Calendar of Prayer* issued by the national office of the United Church Board for World Ministries. Though no answers are expected, it is amazing how often letters with exotic stamps find their way to the colonial-style church, expressing the gratitude of missionaries for this prayer support.

What an important partnership this is! I reaffirm a commitment to remain faithful, supporting missionaries like Bernard, who bring good tidings to all people.

Our Father God who loves four-footed animals as well as two-footed, we thank you for the occasional partnership that teams these creatures of God to assist wayfarers, travelers, and those in need of spiritual sustenance. Help us to do our part in this great endeavor, that your love and your message may reach the lowest and the highest parts of the earth; in Jesus' name. Amen.

Living Well

Life lived short or long

*Let the mountains bear
prosperity for the people.*
    —Psalm 72:3 (RSV)

When I drove into the Swiss Alps in Europe, I thought about the tiny blossoms I had seen in the Rocky Mountains of America, where similar flowers dotted the mountain meadows. There were larkspur, roses, crocus, and foxglove, along with buds that eventually would become strawberries and raspberries. As the van shifted into low gear and labored around the increasingly steep turns, gentian and azalea lined the road beside yellow and white edelweiss, the national flower of Switzerland.

The many little plants grew tenaciously and flowered profusely, though the season was short and the environment difficult. They did their best to reflect the Creator's plan in the few short days or weeks allowed them, producing flowers and fruit to cheer and sustain the hardy mountaineers. The paslmist's words echoed in my ears—"Let the mountains bear prosperity for the people."

Once home amid the daily routine, the memory of those short-lived plants faded, until a young acquaintance died. She had been a reporter for our local daily newspaper, and at thirty-three, her life was ended. Barbara Van Nice had aplastic anemia, a rare blood disease for which there is no cure. Yet I, who dropped into the newsroom regularly with completed assignments, never knew it. She always greeted me with a friendly Hello, and not once did she indicate that her days were numbered.

Later I learned from her editor, Bill Breisky, that she was an excellent newspaperwoman. As copy editor, she watched over the production of the paper, wanting each issue to be the best possible. Her fellow reporters had a phrase for a story given Barbara's treatment: "It's been Van Nice-ized." In an editorial, Bill wrote, "Her extraordinary dedication to truth is bound to make exceptional journalists out of those of her fellow workers who have been inspired by her example. . . . Her courage and grace and humor will live as long as her friends."

Inevitably, I contrasted Barbara's life with those of others who had lived much longer but not nearly as well. They had simply marked time in the relentness march from the cradle to the grave.

In retrospect, I am grateful for a short life lived well. Barbara was like those mountain flowers who seized their opportunity, grew, flourished, and produced. In the life-span allotted her, she brought enjoyment to others with her quiet, pleasing ways, and she brought the fruits of good production to her calling.

I reflect that it is not how long one lives, but how well those years are lived that is important. Barbara would have empathized with Justice Oliver Wendell Holmes, who had a similar outlook, though he was granted a much longer life-span. When President Roosevelt asked why he was reading Plutarch's *Lives* at the age of ninety-two, Holmes replied, "To improve my mind."

Our Father, God of tiny flowers and plants as well as of humans, help each of us to fulfill the mission you have assigned to us. Give us strength and wisdom to live to the full each year of our lives and to do our allotted tasks to your glory; in Jesus' name. Amen.

The Signal

*All you inhabitants of the world,
you who dwell on the earth,
when a signal is raised on the mountain, look!*
—Isaiah 18:3 (RSV)

Periodically, God seems to send a signal to humans through the natural world.

One of the most recent was the cataclysmic eruption of Mount Saint Helens, in the state of Washington. At 8:32 A.M. on May 18, 1980, that gleaming white volcanic peak blasted away 1,300 feet of its crest, in a massive eruption with the fury of a ten-megaton bomb. Two hundred square miles of the northwest were devastated and 61 lives lost.

To those of us who watched on television it was an awesome experience. But our feelings were nothing as compared to the emotions it evoked among those who monitored the rumbling volcano, those who actually experienced the monstrous electric storm that followed, or those who lived for weeks amid falling volcanic ash.

Rowe Findley, assistant editor of *National Geographic Magazine,* who had been observing the rumbling volcano, wrote in the January 1981 issue,

The very beauty of the mountain helped to deceive us. It was a mountain in praise of mountains, towering over lesser peaks, its near perfect cone glistening white in all seasons. . . . Thousands through the years had given it their hearts—climbers, artists, photographers, lovers of beauty's ultimate expression. . . . For all its splendor, Mount St. Helens was a time bomb, ticking away toward a trigger labeled "self-destruct."

I wondered often in succeeding days about the meaning of such a cataclysmic event—especially as reports came in of

150-foot trees scattered like straw, of houses swept away, of the death of people and animals.

The verse from Isaiah came to mind. "When a signal is raised on the mountain, look!" Was this event a signal? And if so, of what?

I discounted punishment, for I do not believe God sends these happenings as punishment to humans. Sometimes, though, we punish ourselves with natural calamities, such as the Dust Bowl of mid-America. When we rape the earth, we receive retribution.

No, it seems this disaster was a result of the earth's movements. Our world's crust is a series of plates, which slip and slide over an interior hot, viscous sea. As these plates grind past or slide beneath one another at the rate of eight inches a year, the magma of melting rock below finds its way upward in volcanic action.

My best understanding of this signal came from Findley, after he had flown over the devastated area. "More than a fear for personal safety, I felt a growing apprehension for all of us living on a planetary crust so fragile, afloat atop such terrible heats and pressures. Never again, it came to me then and remains with me to this day, would I regain my former complacency about this world we live on."

Perhaps this natural calamity and others like it are meant to make us realize that life here is transitory and that to feel secure in this world, we must be at home in the next—which is closer than breathing, nearer than hands or feet. It is as permanent and safe as our current passage in this world is transitory and fleeting.

When a signal is raised on a mountain, look!

Dear Father of both worlds, we thank you for the beauty and wonder of this earth. Help us to refrain from becoming so engrossed in its activities that we neglect our spiritual lives.

Draw us nearer to you so we may live both in the here and in the hereafter; in Jesus' name. Amen.

Change, A Fact of Life

Therefore we will not fear though the earth should change, though the mountains shake in the heart of the sea.
—Psalm 46:2 (RSV)

It was the glorious changing pattern of light in the canyons and cliffs of the Southwest that taught me about a seemingly changeless natural world that is constantly changing. Furthermore, I learned that this change is a part of God's plan.

My husband had pulled our house trailer down a number of hairpin turns into Zion National Park in Utah. We were parked on a grassy plot by a swift-flowing crystal-clear stream. While the rest of the family explored, I relaxed in a lawn chair, gazing almost vertically upward at the sharp, rainbow-tinted cliffs. As the sun slowly crossed the deep-blue sky, the canyon walls were a palette of constantly changing colors—from dark red and orange to light purple and pink.

I thought about change, not only on the surface but beneath, where alterations in mountains and canyons are measured in thousands of years. Those walls looked absolutely undisturbed, yet geologists tell us there is continual erosion and movement. As James Michener said in *Centennial*, "The earth was at work, as it is always at work."

Even the great physicist Albert Einstein accepted change. "There are no eternal theories in science. . . . Every theory has its period of gradual development and triumph after which it may experience a decline." Late in life, Einstein confessed that he had come to regard his own theory of relativity as inadequate, though he felt he was too old at that time to undertake the effort to rethink it.

I mused about change in humans. When I was young I believed the universe was governed by a series of fixed laws. Did the sun not always rise in the east and set in the west? The cycle of the seasons came and went with unvarying precision. Like the natural world, humans too had patterns. We grew, learned, chose a life work or a life partner (sometimes both), and stayed on a prescribed path until retirement.

But as I matured, I found that those patterns are not always followed. Though there are natural laws that govern the universe and moral laws that govern humans, within this framework there is constant change. In fact, God expects it. He wants us to expand and grow.

I watched the ever-changing light play on the face of the seemingly unchanging face of Zion's West Temple Cliff directly before me. The shades were growing darker as the sun began its downward journey. I thought of the words of H. G. Wood: "Contemplation of the living world, of its diversity and beauty brings to many a unique feeling of nearness of God. We now see creation as a process, involving numberless converging and diverging lines of development, still active, but inconceivably slow."

I could understand why the early Mormon settler named this particular escarpment West Temple: It evoked a reverent mood. I felt a strange benediction, almost a sense of relief as the certainty swept over me that change is a natural fact of life. In fact, it is a process that is expected of us.

God of the ever-changing universe, help us to anticipate eagerly the opportunities for change in our own lives. When these appear, help us to step forth in faith and meet the challenges, conscious that you are with us. We thank you for supporting the forces of change in the natural, as well as in the human world; in Jesus' name. Amen.

Layers

*They go up by the mountains;
they go down by the valleys
unto the place which thou hast founded for them.*
—Psalm 104:8

We are indebted to James Michener's *Centennial* for a vivid description of the earth's structure. At the center, 770 miles in diameter, is "a ball of solid material very heavy and incredibly hot." Around this core, there is a thick fluid, movable but not liquid, extending 1,375 miles toward the surface. Next are 1,784 miles of a rock mantle called magma. It is this material which occasionally thrusts upward through the earth's two-mile crust to form lava, then granite.

Thus the earth's outer shell, which we think of as solid and unmoving, actually is a series of layers and stratas. As the magma intruded, the earth's covering became "wrenched, compressed, eroded and savagely distorted by cataclysmic forces." This action produced the mountains and valleys of today. Where erosion by rain and wind has revealed sharp escarpments, travelers in mountains and canyons can see these varied layers. I recall staring in fascination at one ledge of the Grand Canyon in Arizona where strips of slate gray, sand tan, charcoal black, and an unbelievable pink lay twisted and folded.

In these later years I have often thought about comparable layers and stratas in humans. I have been intrigued by the Oriental view, which describes life as having three stages (or layers). First is the student period when a person grows and learns. In the worker stage, which follows, one assumes responsibility for the extended family, laboring for food, shelter, and other amenities. Finally, say our Eastern friends, comes the time of fulfillment. Younger folks pick up the burdens, and the elders are free to enjoy experiences for which they often have longed. One person might write poetry or do calligraphy. Another might learn to play the flute or meditate quietly under a tree. Whatever activity brings the most enjoyment and fulfillment is open to them.

Psychologist Carl Jung, writing along these same lines, felt that life has but two stages.

Man's spiritual nature helped give a "sense of meaning" to life. In the first half of life, meaning is concerned with the establishment of self, fulfillment of biological needs, and achievement of a place in society. In the second half, the sphere of meaning shifts to a goal of inner understanding. The later years are more numinous. In old age I have had the experience of being gripped by something that is stronger than myself, something people call God.

I am in the elder class now and can look back over the stages in my life. They were not always level and peaceful. Like those of the Earth Mother, those stages were occasionally fraught with emotional upheavals. Some spots were tilted and upended, others wrenched and distorted. But there also have been plateaus of creativity and emotional satisfaction along the way. I have come to appreciate, especially in later years, the multitude of creative opportunities available to make all our life stages more meaningful.

I can empathize with Jung (whether there are two, three, or perhaps more stages in life). For I have noted, as I traveled my pilgrim trail, that there have been increasing glimpses of something "stronger than myself," something called God. As I have endeavored to fulfill unrealized promises in my genes, I have felt drawn to the place the psalmist says God has founded for us. I am confident that the final strata will not be tilted or convoluted, twisted or folded, but will lead to complete fulfillment.

Our Father who created the mountains and valleys with their varied layers, help us to understand and enjoy the stages in our lives. Enable us to savor each one to the full, as we look forward in anticipation to the next; in Jesus' name. Amen.

One Step at a Time

*Upon the mountain heights of Israel
shall be their pasture.*
—Ezekiel 34:14*b* (RSV)

The problems were really insurmountable, I thought. There were too many projects to be done all at once. Some were held up by road blocks. Others seemed too great for the time available. There were classes to be taught, as well as the necessary preparation; two housing corporations were stalled;

a monthly column was due; a book deadline was looming. To add to the pressure, Thanksgiving was approaching, and a family reunion at my home was imminent.

The way ahead seemed mountainous, with not one crest, but several. How was I to accomplish all this work in just a few short weeks? I thought longingly of the morning Bible reading: "Upon the mountain heights of Israel shall be their pasture." Weren't these mountain heights supposed to be a reward—not a chore?

My mind reverted to my youth and one of my very first attempts to scale a mountain to its heights. My companions and I had set out to climb Mount Chocorua in New Hampshire. It is not a very tall mountain compared to its northern neighbors, so we tackled it with enthusiasm. We started confidently up the trail on a sparkling clear spring day. We stepped lightly through the whispering pines, reveling in the crisp air.

After several hours, however, our steps were not so springy. We puffed and panted with exertion. On reaching the saddle of the mountain, we threw ourselves down on the rocks to rest and drink in the view. Chocorua Lake was a blue jewel below and more mountains had appeared on the northern horizon.

I remember that I turned and glanced upward apprehensively, wondering if I had the stamina to climb that thrust of rock leading to the summit. It was then that our wise leader, probably noting my expression, remarked, "We'll get there if we take it one step at a time."

That experience flashed into my mind recently when I read Hannah Whitehall Smith's helpful book, *The Christian's Secret of a Happy Life*. Hannah Smith, whose book was first published in 1870, was a Quaker. She has been described as "a happy passenger in the chariot of God," and she too talked about one step at a time: "The heights of Christian perfection can only be reached by each moment faithfully following the Guide who is to lead you there: and He reveals the way to us one step at a time, in the little things of our daily lives, asking only on our part that we yield ourselves up to his guidance."

I relaxed, chiding myself for letting the mountains of work ahead loom so large and ominous. I determined to take one step in each project each day, and one day at a time—just as on that long-ago day at Mount Chocorua.

I recalled the words of Sir William Osler, the noted physician:

Banish the future: live only for the hour and its allotted work. Think not of the amount to be accomplished, the difficulties to be overcome, but set earnestly at the little task at your elbow, letting that be sufficient for the day; for our plain duty is not to see what lies dimly at a distance, but to do what lies clearly at hand.

I am revived after this musing. I will not worry about the mountains ahead. I will face today's tasks, hoping eventually to reach the heights.

Gracious Father who gives us tasks to do in life, help us to remember that you are also ready to help us complete them. Give us faith to go forward confidently, trusting you to help us each step of the way; in Jesus' name. Amen.

A Free-flowing Spirit

*He sendeth the springs into the valleys,
which run among the hills. . . .
He watereth the hills from his chambers.*
—Psalm 104:10, 13

One of America's scenic wonders that shall live in my memory is the magnificent waterfall in the Grand Canyon of the Yellowstone in Wyoming. I recall standing on a cliff-edge by those falls, which plunge dramatically one thousand feet to the gorge below. Rainbow shades gleamed from the water and from the canyon walls—predominately gold, but with blends of orange, brown, red, gray, pink, and white. Rock pinnacles and several small geysers added to the breathtaking beauty.

I was awed, not only by this scene of grandeur but by the amount of water cascading blithely over the rocks. Nothing could stop that waterfall. Anything that ventured into its path would be swept over the edge, carried along by the strong current.

Could this be an analogy of the free-flowing Spirit of God when it breaks through our human restraints and bursts into the world? Through the centuries, whenever humans have tried to organize and regulate spiritual activity, a renewed outburst of the Spirit seems to have followed. It is as if God were telling us his Spirit cannot be regimented, but must be free to flow like the water that pours so forcefully over those cliffs.

Thomas Merton, in *Contemplation in a World of Action*, warns us against being too tradition-bound. He urges us instead to be aware of "the currents of uninterrupted vitality" which come from the Infinite. "It is a living spirit marked by freedom and originality." He tells us to "be ready for a new initiative that is faithful to a certain spirit of freedom and of vision which demands to be incarnated in a new and unique situation."

Could this have been in the psalmist's mind when he wrote that God sent springs into the valleys and watered the hills? Often the psalms contain double meanings, so I am content to read that parable into these verses.

There are times when we are well advised to keep within the age-old traditions. But in a world that is changing as rapidly as ours, we must also be ready to receive new dreams and visions to meet differing challenges and activities. I think the psalmist is saying we should so position ourselves that we will be ready channels for God's free-flowing Spirit.

This is not an easy task, but Merton gives us hope.

If we do what we can with the means and grace at our disposal, if we sincerely take advantage of our genuine opportunities, the Spirit will be there and his love will not fail us. . . . Grace has been given us along with our good desires. What is needed is the faith to accept it and the energy to put our faith to work in situations that may not seem to us to be promising. The Holy Spirit will do the rest.

I also take comfort in remembering that God uses humans, however humble, as channels for this Spirit. As George Eliot phrased it in "Stradivarius,"

> Tis God gives skill,
> But not without men's hands: He could not make
> Antonio Stradivarius' violins
> Without Antonio.

Perhaps all that is required of us is that we be faithful, open and waiting, trusting God to send his free-flowing spirit through us into the world, just as he directs those waters in the Grand Canyon of the Yellowstone.

Gracious heavenly Father, we thank you for sending your free-flowing Spirit into the world to liberate our hearts and minds. *We pray that we may always be open channels for this energizing, creative flow; in Jesus' name. Amen.*

On Being Present Where We Are

*Doth the eagle mount up at thy command,
and make her nest on high?
She dwelleth and abideth on the rock,
upon the crag of the rock, and the strong place.*
—Job 39:27

My stapler was misplaced. It was aggravating. I had moved home from my smaller summer quarters, and I needed that stapler for my downstairs study. When I had moved out in June, I had stashed the stapler away where I would be sure to find it in the fall.

Now three months later, either my eyesight or my memory was failing, for the stapler refused to be found. Finally I gave up and bought another. The very next day that perverse stapler appeared on a low bookshelf! It was so positioned that I could have seen it easily from my desk if I had really looked. To be sure, it was gray, somewhat like the color of the wall; but even so, if my eyes had really seen what I looked at, I could have saved the price of a new stapler.

How like life this is, I mused, remembering times when I had been oblivious to the meaning of some scene enacted before my unseeing eyes. How often our minds are on other things and are not really present where we are.

Mountaineers can give us lessons in being acutely aware of our surroundings at every moment, as did Rob Taylor, in *The Breach:*

> Freed by mountains, my spirit soared ever higher above the ranges in joy, held aloft by the wonders they showed me. Yet ever alert did I keep my mind for the safety of my body, never allowing it to be overwhelmed, never intoxicated by the mountain's irresistible lure and beauty. With time, the shivering, blinding fear of my youth became reverence and respect for all one encounters in high places. The crumbling ridge of rock, the howling blizzard fast approaching, the deep-blue crevice lurking beneath the snow-covered glacier all demand utmost clear thinking and decisive action. Only restraint, vigilance and agility separate a life of continued happiness from one of perpetual remorse.

It is as true of ourselves as it is of mountaineers, I thought. And I recalled Quaker educator Douglas Steere's admonition when he spoke to the Australia Yearly Meeting of the Religious Society of Friends, that we should be present where we are:

> How much interior emigration there is all about us: Students emigrate to the future and are not present where they are. Displaced persons live in the past and refuse to let go to the new homeland and to live where they are. Parents are not present here and now but are living for the day when the children are raised, or when they will retire, or when they will be free of this and that, but remain numb and glazed and absent from the present moment.

Steere also reminded me that "to be present is to be vulnerable, to be able to be hurt, to be willing to be spent—but it is also to be awake, alive, engaged actively in the immediate assignment that has been laid upon us."

I must not be so preoccupied that I cannot see what is in front of me, I told myself. I must not miss a call to lend a helping hand to someone. I must not be oblivious to a nudge from the Spirit. I must be like the eagle who mounts up at God's command.

Maybe then I will not misplace any more staplers!

Our heavenly Father, as we go through life, enable us to put aside fears for the morrow and regrets for yesterday. Give us clear vision for the present, so that every moment of every day, we may be alert to your call; in Jesus' name. Amen.

Barrier? Or Pathway?

And I will make all my mountains a way.
—Isaiah 49:11 (RSV)

Until very recent times, the coastal mountains that edge the Pacific Coast in the province of British Columbia, Canada, were largely unexplored. The jumbled, almost pathless mountains, covered with ice fields and pierced by deep canyons, create a barrier 950 miles long, varying in width from 35 to 100 miles. These outcroppings are so menacing that early explorers and latter-day travelers found it much easier to detour. This habit of bypassing the range was so widespread that even today the population is huddled in the lower half of the province near the city of Vancouver.

After visiting the area, author Ralph Gray commented, in *America's Magnificent Mountains:*

Hardly anyone I encountered in Vancouver had heard of Mount Waddington, the highest mountain that juts 13,177 miles in the air and is only 175 air miles northwest of the city. It was as though the "north shore mountains" had been put there merely as a scenic backdrop for the city. What lay beyond was as remote and unknown as Tibet.

Yet within the confines of this range lie millions of acres of forest, where mixed conifers could supply lumber for homes and pulp for paper. King and sockeye salmon crowd the glacial rivers. There are unparalleled opportunities for recreation.

Perhaps this barrier is a proper one. There should be some places in our world where wild things are left alone to thrive and where nature follows the seasons untroubled by the machinations of humans.

Yet I wonder if barriers like this are not unlike some seemingly closed doors in our lives. Sometimes our chosen pathway becomes blocked—the direction we have chosen leads to a stone wall. Will we accept this barrier and turn away discouraged from our dream?

Or will we look more closely to see if there is a pathway around the barrier?

One of the people who refused to let barriers remain is Harold Wilke. This foremost expert on problems and needs of the handicapped was born without arms. Yet he is the very personification of the theme of the recent International Year of Disabled Persons: Full Participation and Equality.

When he was given the Global Citizen Award by the United Church Board for World Ministries in 1981, it was noted that Dr. Wilke has "ministered in a suburban pastorate, in a university chapel, and in armed forces hospitals. For 20 years he directed his denomination's Council for Church and Ministry." He is a member of the President's Committee on Employment of the Handicapped and has worked to mainstream the handicapped in forty countries. He has been a shining example to all of us that barriers can be turned into pathways.

I read recently that those coastal mountains in British Columbia have begun to be less of a barrier. In fifteen stations and twenty lesser camps there, scientists are amassing information about glacial environment that will be invaluable in forecasting changes in world climate. At the Garibaldi Provincial Park and in the Black Tusk Area, backpackers and campers are finding challenges in the vast wilderness. At Tweedsmuir Provincial Park, which encompasses two million acres on the eastern side of the range, there is a work-training program for teenagers.

It seems clear that, like the Alps and the Rockies, these coastal mountains are becoming less a barrier and more a pathway, perhaps symbolic of what can happen in our own lives.

Our heavenly Father who has set the mountains in their places, remain close to us when we come up against stone walls and closed doors in our lives. Help us to see that a seemingly insurmountable barrier is sometimes only an invitation to find a way around that obstacle, or perhaps a new pathway in another direction; in Jesus' name. Amen.

An Alpine Visage

*For the hand of the Lord
will rest on this mountain.*
—Isaiah 25:10 (RSV)

In 1980 I was privileged to experience the world-famous Passion Play in Oberammergau, Germany. I recall driving into the little community nestled on a plain, surrounded by the tall mountains of the Bavarian Alps. I wandered with the rest of our party through the picture-postcard village, enjoying the sight of houses decorated with paintings, the balconies hung with flowers. Then we entered the five-thousand seat Passion Theater and completely forgot the fairytale setting as we became engrossed in the play.

The events of the Passion Week of Jesus Christ, from the Palm Sunday reception in Jerusalem to the resurrection on Easter Sunday, unfolded on stage, accompanied by a Mozart score performed by one hundred fifty symphonic instruments and voices. The thrilling performance invoked deep emotions. I was amazed that on the surface I followed the familiar story, but subliminally I was part of the crowd, caught up in the drama.

Later I reviewed the history of the play, which dates from A.D. 1634. The Black Plague was then sweeping through Europe. The villagers had prayed to God, promising to portray the passion of Jesus Christ if their village were spared from the dread disease. The village was so spared, and for generations the inhabitants had kept that pledge, performing the day-long drama once every decade, from June through September. Everyone who takes part is from the village, and all are trained from birth to feel its importance. The strength of character in the faces of the people reveal their dedication to this pledge.

I was reminded of the description of Baron von Hugel, the spiritual director of the English mystic Evelyn Underhill, in her biography by Margaret Cropper:

> There is a memory of an immense spiritual transcendence, a personality at once daunting and attractive, an Alpine quality. Those who cherish memories of him may even be inclined to think first of a volcanic mountain; for he combined rock-like faith, a massive and lofty intellect with the incandescent fervour, the hidden fire of an intense interior life. The piercing black eyes which compelled truth and obtained it, the awe and passion which were felt when the Baron uttered the name of his God, these will not be forgotten by any soul which came under the sphere of his influence.

These magnificent mountains, plus this noble pledge, breed Alpine faces, I decided, as the narrator introduced the final glittering scene and the Allelulias accompanied by crescendo orchestration, thrilled me to the core.

Truly, the hand of the Lord is upon these mountains, I thought. As the performance ended, the audience reaction was muted, not at all like the lively hum that had preceded the play. Each of us wandered off alone, and I stood watching for a while as the players left the stage doors. It was a fitting climax to my day when a sturdy man of indeterminate age, garbed in brown lederhosen and jacket and sporting an alpine hat with a feather, climbed onto a bicycle and rode into the setting sun. His face was a composite of all I had seen: It was as rocklike, yet as vital as the surrounding mountains.

These people are an example to all of us, I mused as I walked toward our rendezvous with the bus. And I thought of A. D. Burkett's words in "If You Will."

> If God can make—of an ugly seed,
> With a bit of earth and air,

    And dew and rain, sunshine and shade—
      A flower so wondrous fair;
    What can He make—of a soul like you,
      With the Bible and faith and prayer,
    And the Holy Spirit—if you do His will,
      And trust His love and care!

Almighty God, creator of noble mountains and of humans with Alpine visages, help us to emulate these lofty peaks and people. Enable us to remain true to your Word, to your faith, and to prayer, that we may display the fervor and rocklike loyalty of true disciples; in Jesus' name. Amen.

Sunrise Without and Within

Break forth into singing, ye mountains.
—Isaiah 44:23b

Sunrise comes to America simultaneously in two places in the state of Maine. Both Mount Katahdin, the peak at the beginning of the Appalachian Trail, and Cadillac Mountain in Acadia National Park have the distinction of welcoming the first rays of the sun to the United States each morning.

I have never climbed Mount Katahdin, but I have stood atop Cadillac Mountain on Mount Desert Island and enjoyed the eagle's-eye view of the natural splendors of coastal Maine. Innumerable islands, granite headlands, glacial lakes, and sea-washed shores were touched with a pink and gold ethereal glow when first light dawned. It was a breathtaking experience that turned to awe as the darkness rose like a curtain, giving way to light.

As the rainbow-tinted rays touched the summits of the peaks and rested on the tips of the spruce, hemlock, and pines, it was as if the whole landscape rejoiced at the coming of the light. As in the days of Isaiah, the mountains seemed to break forth into singing.

Later, descending the winding road that revealed glimpses of natural beauty at every turn, I thought of that other light which rises perpetually—the light within. Quaker mystic George Fox called it the Inner Light. Though sometimes we are not aware of it, this light is as real as the sunlight that touches mountaintops at dawning. But how difficult it sometimes is to encourage that light within.

Not long ago Helen Hole spoke of that Inner Light while addressing the yearly meeting of the Religious Society of Friends. Looking back on her own life from a perspective of seven decades, she realized that

> there is something in each one of us, alas very deeply buried, something more than ourselves, beyond us and our powers, and that something is present in me. It was only considerably later . . . I understood that this was what the early Friends meant by those terms they used over and over again, those metaphors they chose to convey their basic experience when they spoke of the spark that was waiting to be kindled . . . and of the Inward Light which had the capacity to irradiate our lives.

She went on to liken the growth of this light within herself to that of the photographic process.

> The human eye, looking through a telescope, may detect perhaps a score of fairly bright stars, but a ten-hour exposure, let's say, of a photographic plate, will, at the end of that time, show thousands of them too faint to be seen by the naked eye. So we, when we enter his

Presence day after day become like delicate photosensitive plates which almost imperceptibly collect His light.

There is sunrise without and within, I mused, and like that physical sunrise which brings splendor to mountain summits and treetops, the Inner Light should be developed to light many candles in a dark world. It's up to us to remain true to this call, or the candles assigned to us will remain unlighted.

Father of the light of the heavens and the light within, help us to expose ourselves faithfully to you. Enable us to develop the Inner Light, that we may irradiate your love to others; in Jesus' name. Amen.

Toward the Real

*And when he had sent the multitudes away,
he went up into a mountain apart to pray:
and when the evening was come,
he was there alone.*
—Matthew 14:23

Those creative souls who have received inspiration from nature and passed along their finds to us shall ever have my gratitude. One of those souls was Katharine Lee Bates, born in 1859 not far from the town where I now live. Katharine Bates, a native of Falmouth, was educated at Wellesley College and taught American literature there for most of her life. During her varied career as an author she produced thirteen books and many poems.

One exceptional mountain experience was the inspiration for two of her best-known works. She recalled ascending Pike's Peak in Colorado, where the view from the summit was magnificent and the sunrise overwhelming. The whole panorama of "purple mountain majesties" was her inspiration for the poem "America the Beautiful," which later was set to music by Samuel Ward.

I like to think that experience also was responsible for her more reflective poem "Alone into the Mountains."

> All day from that deep well of life within
>   Himself has He drawn healing for the press
> Of folk, restoring strength, forgiving sin,
>   Quieting frenzy, comforting distress.
>
> Shades of evening fall: importunate still
>   They throng Him, touch Him, clutch His garment's hem,
> Fall down and clasp His feet, cry on Him, till
>   The Master, spent, slips from the midst of them
> And climbs the mountain for a cup of peace,
>   Taking a sheer and rugged track untrod
> Save by a poor lost sheep with thorn-torn fleece
>   That follows on and hears Him talk with God.

I feel that creative souls like Katharine Bates, geniuses of the spirit, are not cut off from us by some intellectual gulf, but in some curious fashion are our links with the Infinite. Their works put our thoughts into words when we are unable to formulate the intimations we feel. In a way their accomplishments are ours because they have shared them with us.

Evelyn Underhill, herself a mystic, believed that the lives of these spiritual giants are guarantees of our end. They are "our lovely forerunners on the path toward the Real. They come back to us from an encounter with life's august secret, as Mary came running from the tomb: filled with amazing tidings which they can hardly tell."

On occasion I finger those books on my shelves that report fragments of the invisible world, and I am grateful for their words. I appreciate once again the discipline and love in the lives of those authors who have given us glimpses of eternity.

Our gracious heavenly Father whom we know only dimly now, help us to grow in knowledge of you as we immerse ourselves in the lives of those who have come close to you. Enable us to appreciate their tidings and, as magnets face the North Star, help us to turn always to you; in Jesus' name. Amen.

Disciplines

*It shall come to pass in the latter days
that the mountain of the house of the Lord
shall be established as the highest of the mountains,
and shall be raised above the hills;
and all nations shall flow to it.*
—Isaiah 2:2 (RSV)

Before 1972, no woman had ever stood upon the peak of any of the world's highest mountains. Then Arlene Blum of the United States met Poland's Wanda Rutiewicz, coming down from the 23,000-foot (7,000-meter) summit of Mount Noshaq in Afghanistan. Elated at her success, Wanda embraced Arlene, saying, "Now we must climb an 8,000-meter peak—just us women."

Annapurna I, in Nepal, was their choice. At 26,504 feet (8,078 meters) it is the world's tenth-highest mountain. A team of 13 women aided by Sherpa guides and porters set out for its summit in August of 1978.

"All are likely to succeed—if anyone makes it—for the Himalayas demand absolute teamwork," read the caption under a picture of the "Annapurna High Class of '78" in the March 1979 *National Geographic Magazine.* Absolute discipline was also required, I deduced, after reading team-leader Arlene's gripping story. Not only were those women well disciplined in their personal lives, but their team discipline was outstanding as they climbed to five separate camps, constantly in touch by radio.

But the teamwork and discipline paid off. The summit was conquered on October 15. Their joy was later tempered with sorrow, for through a mishap on an icy precipice, two of the party lost their lives.

I have sometimes thought that such climbs are so often like our own journey of the spirit. It too is based on teamwork, as we seek to work with God and become channels of his Spirit. But we will not achieve our own personal summits unless we maintain disciplines. Additionally, these should be determined and imposed upon ourselves, similar to the disciplines of the women who climbed Annapurna I.

Elizabeth O'Connor, one of our present-day mystics, in *Our Many Selves,* likens our spiritual disciplines to those of the athlete "whose rigorous program causes him the pain of conditioning and stretching muscles." We too should expect some pain, some darkness of the soul, as we move into these disciplines, she infers. But she cautions that "the disciplines of the athlete, the financier, the musician, the student, are much easier to understand than those of the man who wants to climb a mountain inside himself."

I agree. Outer disciplines—Yoga exercises or diet plans—are much easier to sustain than those necessary for my spiritual progression.

I find the variety of disciplines confusing. Shall I keep a prayer journal? How about carefully studying the lives of mystics? Should I allot a percentage of time for working with others? Shall I tithe in order to aid the world's hungry? Shall I increase my prayer periods? Perhaps I should tackle a progressively more complex reading list?

One thing I do know. Like those women who reached the summit of Annapurna I, I cannot be content without climbing. As Isaiah noted long ago, the house of the Lord shall be established as the highest of the mountains and all nations shall flow to it. Something draws us ever upward.

Harry Kemp, Cape Cod's Poet of the Dunes, expressed this urge in "God, the Architect."

> But chief of all thy wondrous works,
> Supreme of all thy plan,
> Thou hast put an upward reach
> In the heart of Man.

Our Father God, we thank you for the upward urge you have placed in each of us. Help us to design those disciplines that will enable us to climb the heights, and give us strength to be faithful to them and to you; in Jesus' name. Amen.

New Life out of Devastation

*The hay appeareth,
and the tender grass sheweth itself,
and the herbs of the mountain are gathered.*
—Proverbs 27:25

A year after Mount Saint Helens blew her top, Rowe Findley, assistant editor of *National Geographic Magazine,* returned for a look at that massive mountain and the destruction it had wrought. More than 230 square miles of lumber still lies in tangles though there is a massive salvage operation in progress. Beautiful Spirit Lake has disappeared. Lava and mineral ash are everywhere.

Yet amazingly, there is new growth, Findley reported in the December 1981 issue. Pristine lilies, ancient symbols of the Resurrection, bloom amid charred tree stumps. Trailing blackberry, pearly everlasting, lupine, and bracken fern are helping to heal the earth. Moreover, scientists report a prodigious explosion of algae and bacterial life.

Dr. John Baross, microbiologist from Oregon State University, found bacteria on the rocks in the crater. "They must be living on chemistry alone," he said. "There's nothing organic to sustain them."

How amazing to find life amid such desolation, I mused, putting down the article. My mind reverted to a visit we had made to an ancient lava cone in the American West. After climbing an ebony trail, we stood on a small hill. Black rock stretched as far as we could see. Yet I do recall spots of green in that desolate lunarlike landscape. Spears of new growth were pushing upward through the dark crevices.

God never gives up, I thought, with either the physical universe or the human family. I remembered the Prison Fellowship bulletin I had received that day. Charles Colson (one of President Richard Nixon's team, you may recall) had become a born-again Christian and had founded the Prison Fellowship. One of its aims is to "exhort and assist the Church of Jesus Christ in the prisons and in the community" in its ministry to prisoners and ex-offenders, and to their families. Remarkable results have taken place, even on death row, where desperate beings have been reborn. In 1981 there were 229 in-prison seminars, 200 community caring groups, 3,000 match-ups between prisoners and friends on the "outside." The work has spread to other countries. Some Christians have taken Christ's call to minister to those in prison seriously. Others, who have been unable to minister personally, have sent money.

One prisoner, Evamarie Graham, wrote, "I rejected Christ when my daughter died. I went so far as to curse the Lord and tried to shut Him out of my life. But His love and His power is so great, He has pulled me under his wing." Out of desolation has come new life!

Langdon Gilkey, who was incarcerated in the Far East during World War II, described his experiences in *Shantung Compound*.

One of the strangest lessons that our unstable life-passage teaches us is that the unwanted is often creative rather than destructive. No one wished to go to Weihsien Camp. Yet, such an experience, resisted and abhorred, had within it the seeds of new insight and thus of new life for many of us. Almost because of its discomfort, its turmoil and its boredom, it eventually became the source of certainties and of convictions with which life could be more creatively faced.

I thought back over unwanted circumstances in my own life. Those were not the terrible events they first had seemed. God's grace had given strength to overcome, circumvent, and triumph over those hard places. Maybe that is what he tries to tell us when we see new life amid devastation.

Heavenly Father who watches tenderly over each of us, enable us to work creatively through the hard trials of life. Give us strength to triumph and a firm faith, whatever comes; in Jesus' name. Amen.

A Spiral of Prayer

He sendeth the springs into the valleys, which run among the hills.
—Psalm 104:10

Yoesemite National Park, on the western slopes of the Sierra Nevada Mountains in California, is one of America's wonderlands. I remember coming out of Wawona Tunnel into cliff-bound Yosemite Valley and being confronted with a dazzling view of sparkling Bridal Veil Falls, dropping downward into the sheer-walled valley. Speechless for a few moments, I gazed at the vast expanse—then watched, mesmerized, as the dancing waters coursed over the rocks into the Merced River en route to the Pacific Ocean.

I compared that sparkling clear water with the turgid rivers we had passed on our way. How wonderfully clear and wholesome are these mountain springs before they become contaminated by the populace in crowded cities.

"He sendeth the springs into the valleys," ran like a refrain through my mind. The psalmist, too, must have noted that when God originated these springs they were clear and clean—healthful waters for humans and animals. It is only later that these same waters become contaminated.

As I turned away to seek out more vistas in the huge park, I mused on the contrast between ourselves and these waters, for we proceed in the opposite direction. We are like the muddy downstream waters—but unlike them, we have a deep desire to struggle upstream and become more clean. We long to be purified; to be like the waters that spring from the hills.

Margaret Harmon Bro put the simile well, in *More Than We Are:*

> Over and over again as we ascend the spiral of prayer we have to keep reminding ourselves of our sure intent. Our purpose is to know God by expelling from our being all elements that are foreign to his nature. We are like a drop of water impregnated with impurities but resolved upon becoming purified. If we sound presumptuous in aspiring to his nature, it is only because our longing makes us bold to take him at his word. "Beloved now ye are the sons of God and it doth not yet appear that ye shall be."

I am intrigued by her words "ascend the spiral of prayer." That is what we Christians are constantly attempting, and that ascent is much harder than the descent of the dancing waters on Yosemite's cliffs. But we are different from the natural world. As we have been given more, so more is required of us. Thus unlike Yosemite's waters, we continually strive to be better than we are. We seek to become purer, unadulterated, no matter how difficult the way.

It is so easy, I think, to give up when the way is hard. It is at such discouraging times that I recall Grace Noll Crowell's poem "Pilgrimage."

> Be with me for the way is long and lonely,
> I am bewildered, and I cannot see,

But Lord, I shall not be afraid if only
You walk with me.

If I can ever keep recalling
The darkened roads I traveled in the past
How, after You long guarded me from falling,
Light shone at last:

Then surely, Lord, I can go forward knowing
That somewhere on the hills the light will dawn,
And I shall reach it safely if, in going,
You still lead on.

God of the springs and the streams, thank you for their example of purity. Help us in our struggle up the spiral of prayer to become as pure as they, to become your worthy disciples; in Jesus' name. Amen.

The Hill Difficulty

*I cried unto the Lord with all my voice,
and he heard me out of his holy hill.*
—Psalm 3:4

One of the famous high lands in literature is hill Difficulty, found in *Pilgrim's Progress*. Christian, who felt convicted of sin, had forsaken family and friends in the City of Destruction to seek the Celestial City. After having traversed the Slough of Despond and overcoming other trials, he now was faced with hill Difficulty. He was perplexed because "there were also in the same place two other ways besides that which came straight from the gate; one turned to the left, and the other to the right, at the bottom of the hill; but the narrow way lay right up the hill and the name of that going up the side of the hill is called Difficulty."

After refreshing himself with a drink at the nearby spring, Christian started up the hill, saying,

> The hill, though high, I covet to ascend;
> The difficulty will not be offend,
> For I perceive the way of life lies here.
> Come, pluck up, heart, let's neither faint nor fear.
> Better, though difficult, the right way to go,
> Than wrong, though easy, where the end is woe.

I have often pondered John Bunyan's allegory, written while he was confined in prison for preaching the gospel and failing to attend the parish church. I think of hill Difficulty especially when I am tempted to take a shortcut. There are times when a detour around a problem is faster and better. There are other times when the shorter, lower way to reach a goal is simply wrong.

Christian's two companions Formalist and Hypocrisy discovered this fact. When they saw that the hill was steep and high, they decided to take the easier sideroads. "Now the name of one of the ways was Danger and the other Destruction. So the one took the way called Danger, which led him into a great wood; and the other took up directly the way of Destruction, which led him into a wide field, full of dark mountains, where he stumbled and fell, and rose no more."

How am I to know when the climb up hill Difficult is the only way to go? Fortunately, I found comfort and guidance in *Newness of Life,* in the words of Estelle Carver.

To acknowledge the authority of Jesus to govern, to trust his wisdom to guide, to receive him and thus welcome all the doings and happenings of our lives as opportunities for praising and blessing his holy name—these are lessons that must be mastered if we are to grow in newness of life. . . . It is therefore imperative that all who would walk in newness of life keep on asking, seeking and knocking until God's direction and rule are evident in all departments of our lives.

As the poet John Oxenham observed in "The Ways,"

> To every man there openeth
> A Way, and Ways, and a Way.
> And the High Soul climbs the High Way,
> And the Low Soul gropes the Low.
> And in between, on the misty flats,
> The rest drift to and fro.
> But to every man there openeth
> A High Way and a Low.
> And every man decideth
> The Way his soul shall go.

Choices are bound to come, I realize, but if we live close to the eternal and open our hearts to the Holy Spirit who transforms, we will be guided on the right path.

God of the high ways, help us to discern our proper direction. When hill Difficulty looms, strengthen us to climb and surmount it. Then lead us to the Celestial City; in Jesus' name. Amen.

Oneness

Let the hills be joyful together.
—Psalm 98:8b

I have been thrilled with the reports of church growth coming out of China in recent months. After a decade of persecution, the church, in this nation containing one-fourth of the world's population, not only has survived but is stronger than ever. Secret "house churches" held Christians together during the cultural revolution.

According to *A.D.* magazine's August 1981 issue, more than 100 churches have reopened in China, and church members number well over a million. In Peking a congregation of 1,000 witnessed the baptism of 84 people on Easter. In Sian, the city where Christianity was introduced by Nestorians in the seventh century, the reopened church has three Sunday services, with 500 seated inside and just as many standing outside at each service. The same enthusiastic reports come from Canton, Hangshou, and Shanghai.

There is a full complement of students at the Protestant seminary in Nanjing. The school also produces a correspondence course in theology for students in rural areas. To this date, 30,000 copies of the course have been printed.

I am particularly struck by the fact that the church in China has emerged without denominations. Its suffering has given it the gift of unity. Bishop K. H. Ting thinks the Chinese church is in a unique period of transition, much as the European churches were during the Reformation. Those who are concerned about Christianity's future should take note, he says. "Ours may be considered a sort of laboratory whose experiments they cannot afford to miss."

I cannot help feeling that this oneness is God's way of reaching out to us, for unity always has been stressed in the Bible and in nature. My mind goes back through the years to an afternoon spent on a mountain trail. We were deep in the woods on a sunny day. The trees and the underbrush were a verdant green. There was a hush as the sun filtered through the leaves, giving the effect of a stained-glass window. Wild flowers dressed in many colors seemed to nod as we passed by. No one spoke in that natural cathedral. I felt a pull of the heart as a startled chipmunk faded into the greenery. I sensed a current of life that included all of nature, as well as myself. A oneness in the universe enveloped me.

Fran Giles, in *Union Life* magazine, told of a similar feeling experienced on a nature trail.

Joy sprang up. . . . I was so full of joy and understanding that I had an expectancy growing up within me almost like a spring that was about to be opened up to gush out and pour over the roads, the fields, flowers, grass, cows, farms, and mountains. I realized at the same time that the oneness was springing up in all those surrounding things to overflow me, and it was in a continuous eternal spring in me, in all manifestations of God.

As I emerged from that forest trail long ago and came upon a view of hills rising in ranks in the distance, I thought of the verse in the Psalms, "Let the hills be joyful together."

There is nothing on earth that compares with the majesty of God as he expresses himself in nature, I mused. Everything living joins the eternal hills in reaching upward in praise. But even more, this praise invades us all, for we are all one.

As Dante wrote in his *Divine Comedy,*

> I raised my eyes aloft, and I beheld
> The scattered chapters of the Universe
> Gathered and bound into a single book
> By the austere and tender hand of God.

Our Father, Father of all things animate and inanimate, help us to appreciate the unity you have designed into our universe. Help us further to recognize that Christians, and indeed all humankind, will not fully realize the potential you have in store for us until we know that we are citizens of one world and that all are part of you; in Jesus' name. Amen.

In, But Not of, The World

*On this mountain the LORD of hosts
will make for all peoples a feast.*
—Isaiah 25:6 (RSV)

"Most people are *on* the world, not *in* it. [They] have no conscious sympathy or relationship to anything about them," said John Muir, that giant among conservationists.

As I think back on my mountain experiences, I know what he means. If ever I have been too long without a trip into the wilderness, I become too easily concerned with surface living. I need to be reminded often that I am kin to the elemental wilderness and that my roots need to go deeply into it.

William O. Douglas, another lover of unspoiled natural areas of the world, and a disciple of Muir, observed the importance of getting back to nature, in *My Wilderness:*

Nature builds strength and character competitively. Domesticated animals, like men and women of cities, get lazy habits. They become dependent on others losing the drive and initiative that marked the beginning of the species. . . . This loss of character can be disastrous to a race of men who, apartment-born, never experience the challenge that nature demands of all her children. This race of apartment-born people is of the earth, yet not a vital part of it. It is coddled and protected, utterly dependent on machines for its existence. It does not know how to pit human ingenuity against the universe; it therefore has no key to survival against disaster.

Wilderness is important, then, I thought as I read those words, not just as an object for appreciation, but as a must for living to the fullest capacity. Douglas continued,

Men need testing grounds to develop these capacities. They cannot flower at Coney Island or at the ball park. Men need to know the elemental challenges that sea and mountains present. . . . They need to unlock the secrets of streams, lakes and canyons and to find how these treasures are veritable storehouses of inspiration. They must find a peak or ridge that they can reach under their own power alone.

It is when we reach those heights, I mused, remembering my own thrill on reaching my first mountaintop, that we find a balcony for overlooking the world and a springboard for leaping into God's mysterious other world. It is as if we have our feet on the pulse of this world, while our hearts are stretching into the next.

And yet I remember an overpowering feeling that I was not really stretching out to God. Rather, he was reaching down to me and I was but responding to him. We sense this more surely on a mountaintop than at any other place. Was that what Isaiah felt when he said, "On this mountain the Lord of hosts will make for all peoples a feast"? I am sure he referred to a spiritual feast—sustenance for the growth of our souls.

An unknown author had this same feeling long ago:

> I sought the Lord, and afterward I knew
> He moved my soul to seek Him, seeking me;

It was not I that found, O Saviour true,
No, I was found of Thee.

Thou didst reach forth Thy hand and mine enfold;
I walked and sank not on the storm-vexed sea,—
'Twas not so much that I on Thee took hold,
As Thou, dear Lord, on me.
—"I Sought the Lord"

God of this world and of the next, we praise you for eternally calling us to be one with thee. Help us to take time away from common days to experience the uncommon ones in nature, so that we may respond to your ever-loving call and feast on your riches; in Jesus' name. Amen.

On Moving Mountains

*If ye have faith as a grain of mustard seed,
ye shall say unto this mountain,
remove hence to yonder place;
and it shall remove;
and nothing shall be impossible unto you.*
—Matthew 17:20*b*

Jesus' statement that we can have faith great enough to move mountains has always baffled me. I long to have such faith, yet I feel sure that even with much prayer and fasting, I could not move an Alp.

Then I read a *Christian Science Monitor* article, "Moving

Mountains," in which we are advised to start with something less formidable.

There are Christians of many denominations who have practically applied this Biblical promise to other kinds of problems that rise mountainlike in an otherwise smooth and steady life. Take for example red tape.

Most of us have been confronted by mountains (or even mountain ranges) of red tape in government forms, business procedures and so forth. The problem plagues many societies. But our Master lovingly assures us that faith can move those mountains.

I thought immediately of the housing complexes our United Church of Christ lay people had produced on Cape Cod, in concert with government funding. There were many times when we yearned to give up. The mountain of red tape, particularly for those first eighty-three units for elderly folk in Falmouth, seemed insurmountable. But persistence and faith paid off, and eight years after the inception of the idea, grateful seniors moved in. The red tape had not diminished with succeeding projects, but our faith had increased and mountains had been moved.

The *Monitor's* article noted, "Mountainous problems of any kind are results of mistaken belief that creation is matter-structured. The binding, confusing, or delaying of legitimate action results from thought that is tied up with these entangling, false beliefs. Faith frees us."

I have been troubled by the amount of red tape and the burgeoning bureaucracy that faces us. The need for housing is desperate, yet since we first began to fill this need in 1962, the impediments seemed to have multiplied a thousandfold. Didn't someone say that bureaucracy only breeds more bureaucracy and that it is impossible to streamline it?

It is a comfort to think of Jesus, who in spite of pharisaical red tape and the indignities handed him by governing bodies, persisted in cutting through to help his fellow citizens. I think

Jesus, by example, tells us to keep our hearts open to him, that we may grow in faith and thus move our own mountains.

The poet Francis Quarles must have sensed this several centuries ago.

> Even as the needle that directs the hour,
> (Touched with the loadstone) by the secret power
> Of hidden Nature, points upon the Pole;
> Even so the wavering powers of my soul,
> Touch'd by the virtue of Thy Spirit, flee
> From what is earth, and point alone to Thee.
> —*Emblems*

Our heavenly Father who loves and watches over all aspects of life, help us to grow in faith. Enable us so to keep our minds and hearts on you that we can move the Alps that loom on life's horizon; in Jesus' name. Amen.

Oxygen of the Spirit

*The blessings of thy father have prevailed
above the blessings of my progenitors
unto the utmost bound of the everlasting hills.*
—Genesis 49:26

One of the crucial problems facing climbers in high altitudes is the lack of oxygen. This is probably the main reason the fourteen tallest mountains in the world remained unconquered until recent years. Those Asian monarchs, which rise many thousand feet above sea level in the Himalayas and Karakorams, thwarted all comers until the 1950s. Then in 1953 the summit of Annapurna I was reached by a French expedition, and Sir Edmund Hillary of England and the Nepalese Sherpa guide Tenzing Norkey conquered 29,028-foot Mount Everest.

Hillary, who led the successful assault on Everest, called "high, thin air" one of the barriers to human existence on those rarified heights. Lowell Thomas, in *A Book of the High Mountains,* explained further.

Human lungs and other organs must become acclimated to functioning in the rarified atmosphere encountered at great altitudes. Mountain sickness, dulled reflexes, faulty judgment, emotional instabilities all result from overexposure to insufficient oxygen. Even the use of oxygen tanks is not the final solution, for they contain only a limited supply.

Yet in spite of this and other difficulties, Hillary's party persisted, giving Queen Elizabeth a very special present when it succeeded in conquering the world's highest mountain on the eve of her coronation.

As I read the inspiring story of that tremendous feat, an analogy of the spiritual world flashed into my mind. Just as oxygen is essential to life on the physical plane, so prayer is essential to life in the realm of the spirit. If we hope to climb life's obstacles and problems, prayer is necessary for the ascent. As Teresa of Avila remarked centuries ago, "There is but one road which reaches God, and that is prayer."

Emily Gardner Neal, in her inspiring book *The Healing Power of Christ,* noted this same analogy. "Prayer constitutes the very atmosphere we breathe in the climate of healing; it is the oxygen of the spirit. It is the means by which we establish a relationship with God and the means through which we are enabled to live continually in that relationship."

I have not climbed those Asian monarchs and I never will.

But I have toiled up Mount Washington in New Hampshire, and I have driven through high passes in the Rockies and stopped to explore them. In those places, I have felt the lightening of the air. I have had to move more slowly, breathe more deeply, think more carefully. I realized at those times how precious oxygen is, every moment of every day. Although we take it for granted, it is one of God's continual blessings.

Equally, my soul must have spiritual oxygen—prayer—in good supply to be ready for all life brings. When faced with a complex problem, I must remember to replenish my supply of this spiritual oxygen. Perhaps I should make a weekend retreat. I might observe a day of fasting along with prayer. I am grateful for the spiritual giants of the past and present who witness to the importance of prayer in life.

Our Father who created oxygen for our physical bodies, thank you for showing us how to nourish our spiritual life through prayer. May we ever keep this prayer channel open, so that your Spirit will be always available to give our souls sustenance; in Jesus' name. Amen.

Conquering an Everest

*And the glory of the Lord
went up from the midst of the city,
and stood upon the mountains.*
—Ezekiel 11:23

There was another conquest of Mount Everest. From Katmandu in Nepal, the Ministry of Tourism announced that climbers from a United States medical expedition successfully reached the summit in October of 1981. The twenty-one member party was the first to carry out medical and scientific tests on the mountain.

I was struck by the fact that only a few humans will ever climb a physical Mount Everest, but many are called to scale such heights in their lives. I was deeply touched not long ago by *The World in My Mirror,* written by a woman faced with such an Everest. At seventeen, Margaret Jean Jones had become ill with a mysterious disease that left her almost totally paralyzed.

"Conquering an Everest, strewn with boulders of pain and physical limitations and laced with crevices created by lack of educational opportunities has always been the challenge confronting the handicapped," she writes in her inspiring autobiography. But conquer she did, for in spite of confinement to her bed for the past twenty-two years, she has pursued a writing career and maintained a genuine interest in everything around her. Though she has only partial use of one arm and hand, she writes newspaper columns and books. With the assistance of a mirror wired to her chest, she is able to observe and be part of her surroundings.

Many of us would be in deep depression if we were in Margaret Jones' situation. She refused to give in to self-pity and climbed her Everest, aided by a strong faith, which grew in adversity. She was inspired by the words of Helen Keller: "Sick or well, blind or seeing, bond or free, we are all here for a purpose and, however we are situated, we please God better with useful deeds than with many prayers of pious resignation."

Margaret Jones' deeds have been multitudinous. While stricken with illness she helped organize and raise funds for an activities center in her hometown of Cullman, Alabama. (Later, that center was named for her.) In addition to her column "Through the Looking Glass" and her autobiography, she has written two books of local history and is working on a novel. She says,

I know now that wholeness is not so much in having perfect health as it is in being in harmony with God and in obedience to his will. . . . Not only is Jesus Christ our Lord a stone of help, he is the mortar that bonds the broken pieces of shattered, lonely, sinful, and desperate lives into beautiful mosaics of peace and joy. He is all in all, totally adequate.

I now look at my own life with new eyes. If a person with such a handicap can be so triumphant, can I, who have all my faculties, be less so? No more grumbling over aches and pains. No more fretting when schedules are botched. No more complaining, I tell myself severely, when there are too many duties to fit into too few hours.

I think of Ezekiel, who said that the glory of the Lord stood upon the mountains. I remember the masthead of the *Alabama Wheelchair Society* magazine: "When God closes a door he always opens a window." I will not forget Margaret Jean Jones, no dweller in the lowland, who conquered her Everest and made that glory shine for the rest of us.

Our heavenly Father who knows when a tiny sparrow falls, thank you for the inspiration of handicapped lives that have

climbed to unimaginable heights. Give us the understanding and the will to climb ever upward when such mountains appear in our lives; in Jesus' name. Amen.

Symbols

*Till ye be left as a beacon
upon the top of a mountain,
and as an ensign on an hill.*
—Isaiah 30:17b

Symbols always have intrigued me. Webster's dictionary defines a symbol as "a visible sign of something invisible." The Bible recounts many incidents when a sign was given to remind mortals of a special event or an eternal truth. A rainbow in the sky, a pearl of great price, a mustard seed, a widow's mite—all are visible signs of something invisible.

For Christians, the historic symbol is the cross, a sign of death transmuted by the alchemy of love into an emblem of the living. Ever since the time of Constantine in the early fourth century when it was officially adopted as Christianity's symbol, the cross has captured hearts and imaginations. From Byzantium and Rome, its use spread throughout western Europe, penetrated Africa, and traveled through Asia to India and China. Many and elaborate are the types, from the equal-sided Crusader crosses to the hundreds of variations of the more common elongated shape.

Therefore I was excited to discover that nature has at times produced this same symbol. Between Vail and Red Cliff in Colorado, there is an outcropping called the Mountain of the Holy Cross. If one drives west from Wheeler Junction on a U.S. forest road, one can see why this mountain was so named. Until very recently there was a perfect cross outlined on the mountainside. This resulted from a combination of deep ravines, arranged 1,500 feet vertically and 750 feet horizontally on each side. Since the mountain was 13,977 feet high, the ravines were continually filled with snow, creating a perfect cross. A rock slide has distorted the cross somewhat, but the mountain still highlights this symbol. I have wondered if Isaiah had seen a similar natural phenomenon on snowy Mount Hermon long ago, when he spoke of an ensign on a hill.

One of my pleasures through the years has been to collect crosses in interesting forms. I have one of ornate silver, with the Lord's Prayer in miniature inscribed at the cross beam. Another is made of blue and ivory stained glass. Still another, the form adopted by the Huguenots, has a dove of peace attached. I have watched with interest the increasing number of clergy who are adding crosses to their daily attire as well as to their ecclesiastical robes.

I recall that during the sixteenth century some of the Reformers, in their zeal to return to primitive Christianity, eliminated the symbol of the cross as undesirable. But fortunately, as Dr. John Sutherland Bonnell has pointed out, "The descendants of these reformers came to see that a legitimate use may be made of symbolism . . . as long as it is clear that these symbols are not objects of worship but only reminders of invisible beliefs."

As I write, I finger the inch-high sandstone cross found on the floor of a southern cave. If we tend to forget the message of overpowering love that was epitomized by Jesus and is the basis of our faith, God reminds us of it in unexpected ways. He seems to urge us to become beacons and signs of this love among the world's people.

Our Father who loves us with an undying love, help us to respond to that love. May the symbols of our faith remind us of your caring and inspire us in return to care deeply for others; in Jesus' name. Amen.

Mists

*They are wet
with the showers of the mountains.*
—Job 24:8

The celebrated explorer Henry Stanley was crossing Africa on safari north of Lake Tanganyika when he gazed upward and, to his astonishment, saw a massive mountain range. He had set out across the vast uncharted territory in 1888 to locate the source of the Nile. Instead, he had come across Ruwenzori, the fabled Mountains of the Moon. Natives had reported their existence but no European had sighted them before.

The reason was simple! The range, which is on the equator, has constant heavy rain. High temperatures at the foot of the mountains cause condensation and the resulting clouds almost always hide these mountains of mystery. Fortunately, that day when Stanley was there to observe them, the mists parted. I wonder if Job had heard of those legendary mountains when he spoke of showers on mountains.

I have never seen the Mountains of the Moon, yet I have often thought that they have a remarkable parallel in our lives. We are not always aware of the vast uncharted teritory within our minds and souls. Yet hiding in our subconscious is a rich hinterland, a new unmapped world. Mystics have ventured into this little-known world occasionally, lifting the curtain for the rest of us.

William W. Harman says of this inner land, "When one turns his attention inward, he discovers a vast world of 'inner space' which is as vast and and 'real' as the external physical world. Through exploring this inner world, each one of us potentially has access to vast realms of knowledge through his own mind."

Marilyn Morgan Hellberg is another of today's true spiritual explorers. Believing that many of us have neglected the contemplative part of our Christian heritage, she left her college teaching duties for a year to study the meditation techniques used throughout history. In the April 1980 *Guideposts* magazine, she confessed,

> I hadn't been conscious of the kingdom within because I had been too busy frantically scurrying from one external goal to another. When I prayed, I would direct my attention outward, as if I were sending long distance messages to a remote Being way off in the sky somewhere. . . . Then I started to meditate. I learned to withdraw my attention temporarily from external distractions and to focus deeply inward until I felt I was standing in the presence of God. For the past five years, specific forms of Christian meditation have been a vital part of my prayer life, bringing me heightened awareness, increased perception and alert restfulness.

I felt guilty while reading her words. How true her experience sounded—not because I was praying to a Being "out there," but because I have so often neglected the contemplative aspect of the faith. Like the mists that obscured the Mountains of the Moon, the high values of the inward journey have been set aside by busy schedules. These and a hesitancy to journey into the unknown have hidden the face of God.

Fra Giovanni, a mystic of long ago, understood these human frailties and gently urged us on. "Life is so full of meaning and purpose, so full of beauty beneath its covering—that you will find that earth but cloaks heaven. Courage then to claim it—that is all. But courage you have and the knowledge that we are pilgrims together, wending through an unknown country, home."

Creator of all that exists, thank you for being within us even when we are not really aware of your presence. Give us courage and persistence to delve ever more deeply within and rest more securely in you; in Jesus' name. Amen.

The Intrinsic Value of Beauty

*It is like the dew of Hermon,
which falls on the mountains of Zion!
For there the Lord has commanded the blessing,
life for evermore.*
—Psalm 133:3 (RSV)

One of the most beautiful sights in Japan—yes, even in the world—is the view of Fujiyama (Mount Fuji) on a cloudless day. I was privileged to see that sight some years ago as we sped southwest from Tokyo to Osaka on the bullet train. *Ohs* and *ahs* sounded around me as people glimpsed the peak which appeared to hang in midair. Snow covered the top of the perfect cone while the snowless base was indistinguishable from the similarly tinted gray sky. White streaks spread downward from the notched top, simulating an upside-down Japanese fan.

Today I can still recall the quickening wonder that filled me as I viewed that scene of incredible beauty. I remember similar feelings at other sights of natural beauty, and I have pondered why sheer beauty, like that vision of Mount Fuji, is so important in our lives.

Then in the *Friends Journal,* I came across some words of Rufus Jones, the Quaker mystic who taught earlier in this century.

Everything from a dewdrop to Mt. Shasta is the bearer of beauty and yet beauty has no function nor utility. Its value is intrinsic not extrinsic. It is its own excuse for being. It greases no wheels, it bakes no puddings. It is a gift of sheer grace. . . . It must imply behind things a Spirit that enjoys beauty for its own sake. Where it can break through, it does break through and our joy in it shows we are in some sense kindred to the giver and revealer of it.

How mundane our world would be if we did not have such glimpses of beauty. Perhaps that is the message that comes to us from the psalmist who likens God's blessings to the dew that falls on Zion's mountains. These vistas of incredible loveliness are blessings from God.

I like to think of these glimpses of beauty also as signposts on the way of life, pointing us to the Infinite. This thought occurred to the Evangelical Sisterhood of Mary some years ago. That worldwide organization, born in a revival of young people in Darmstadt, Germany, in 1947, has taken steps to relate scenes of beauty to God. Members have placed plaques of praise in beauty spots of the world. There are such messages on the Noah Monument in Upper Bavaria, on the Grindelwald, first in Switzerland and at an overlook near Steiermark, Austria.

When I visited Canaan in the Desert, their tranquil retreat center in Phoenix, Arizona, the sisters told of plans to put praise plaques at the Grand Canyon and at other American beauty spots. They continually urge others to do likewise. They ask gently, "Everywhere in the world we run into signs of the power of darkness. . . . But where are the signs that call us to God?"

Whether these vistas are labeled or not, they bring us blessings. They call forth from us praise to the Father who created everything for our pleasure and enjoyment, as well as to remind us of him.

God of all beauty in earth and sky, give us eyes to see beyond these earthly vistas to you. Nudge us to set aside times to enjoy the beauty of your world, lest we become caught in the coils of routine living and forget your nearness; in Jesus' name. Amen.

A Rainbow Vista

*The glory of Lebanon shall come unto thee,
the fir tree, the pine tree, and the box together,
to beautify the place of my sanctuary;
and I will make the place of my feet glorious.*
—Isaiah 60:13

There are times when the beauty of this world literally leaves me speechless, struck dumb by its magnitude and scope. Such a time came in Hawaii on a visit to the Island of Molokai. We had flown on a tiny plane to Kalapaupa, the leper colony. The little community is on a small peninsula at the foot of immense cliffs, which for many years shut off contact with the outside world. With the discovery of drugs that effectively control this dread disease, victims can again live out in the world and visitors over sixteen years of age are welcomed to Kalapaupa.

Our host drove us through the small village in its setting of flowers and palm trees. We had tea with the Protestant pastor, chatted with the Roman Catholic priest, and visited several of the residents. Finally we drove to the site of that first austere settlement farther along the coast. Lush green growth covered the cliffs and ran down the valleys like carpeting, meeting the aquamarine sea edged with white pebbles.

Just then a rain shower whisked down the valley and mists clung to the hills. But the sun persisted through the rain and mist until a perfect rainbow arched the heavens. Gradually the mists dissipated, leaving only sunshine and one of earth's loveliest scenes.

The incredible beauty and the symbolism of the rainbow of hope overcoming the storm of dread disease brought a lump to my throat and tears to my eyes. Sometimes earth's beauty overwhelms one.

I was reminded of the poem "God Is Wisdom" by Lois Grant Palches, about another beauty spot.

> Wisely, here
> In old New Hampshire
> God hangs a silver curtain
> Of mists upon the hills, these mornings,
> Lifting it slowly, sensing
> How crowding beauty
> Breaks the heart.

I thought again of the importance of beauty—important not only because it reminds us of the Creator and strikes deeply into our inner core, but because it refreshes us so completely. Better than any tranquilizer is an experience of being immersed in God's glorious world.

Grace Noll Crowell expressed this feeling beautifully in "Summer Fields."

> Here is peace to store within the breast
> Against the days of tumult and despair.
> Within this cool green light the heart can rest,
> The body strengthens in the clear, clean air,
> The soul grows tall, the vio-string tensions cease
> Here in this summer stillness, summer peace.

Creator God who has robed this earth with such splendor, may we ever be conscious of the fir trees, the pine trees, the boxwood, and the beautiful scenes that touch the heart. May our eyes be ever open to them, drinking in the peace, comfort, and quietness our souls so desperately need; in Jesus' name. Amen.

A Symbol of Peace

*Thy steadfast love, O LORD, extends to the heavens,
thy faithfulness to the clouds.
Thy righteousness is like the mountains.*
—Psalm 36:5-6 (RSV)

Christ of the Andes, that huge statue of the Redeemer which stands in the high mountains between Chile and Argentina, must be one of the greatest symbols of peace in the world.

Standing in the Uspallata Pass of the Andes Range in South America, the statue depicts Christ with one hand on a tall cross and the other outstretched toward humanity. It symbolizes the peaceful settlement of a long-standing boundary dispute between the two nations.

In 1881 it was thought the border dispute had been settled when an arbitrary decision fixed the border "along the highest peaks of the Andes." Then in 1890 the exact line became an issue again. There were hotheads on both sides who wanted to settle the issue by force. However, cooler minds prevailed, and with the peacemaking efforts of England's King Edward II, the problem was solved.

To celebrate, the huge statue was erected in the pass near Mendoza. The inscription at the base reads, "Sooner shall these mountains crumble to dust than Argentines and Chileans break the peace sworn at the feet of Christ, the Redeemer."

I reflect on the significance of the fact that Christ, who represented peace and love, was chosen as a symbol of political accord.

I wonder why we do not use more such mediation today, when accord between nations is becoming commonplace in other fields. Scientists from Russia and America sail regularly on friendly missions out of Woods Hole, Massachusetts. Physicians from ideologically opposite countries share medical findings. Writers from Russia and America meet for occasional discussion. Musicians concertize across iron and bamboo curtains. Countries carrying out "cold wars" launch joint ventures into space. Church and synagogue members find sisters and brothers in every nation, race, and color. Why is it not possible to breach political boundaries elsewhere, as in the Andes?

Henry van Dyke, too, must have wondered about this when he wrote "Christ of the Everywhere."

> Christ of the Andes, Christ of the Everywhere.
>   Great Lover of the hills, the open air,
> And patient Lover of impatient men
>   Who blindly strive and sin and strive again,—
> Thou Living Word, larger than any creed,
>   Thou Love Divine, uttered in human need,—
> Oh, teach the world, warring and wandering still,
>   The way to Peace, the footpath of Good Will!

"Do the best you can in the place you are, with the talents you possess"—this was a favorite theme in my husband's sermons. He used to tell of an elderly grandmother in Newton, Massachusetts. Her fingers were crippled with arthritis and she was housebound, yet she knit mittens for the neighboring children and held story hours.

Silently, I determine to follow her example.

God of the rich and the poor, the sick and the well throughout the entire world, help us to be symbols of peace like that great statue of Christ in the Andes Mountains. Enable us to find ways to proclaim your love with acts of friendship and kindness; in Jesus' name. Amen.

A Message Place

*And [Moses] came to the mountain of God,
even to Horeb.*
—Exodus 3:1b

I often wonder about guidance when choices face us. We who follow Christ want very much to tread the pathways in life that would bring God's approval. Yet how do we know which way is right, when two paths confront us? Where can we receive the certainty that the trail we have chosen is the correct one?

It is then I remember Moses. Concerned for his countrymen in bondage in Egypt, he intervened and killed a persecutor. Fleeing Egypt where he had been raised by Pharaoh's daughter, he found refuge in the land of Midian. Settling down as a shepherd and marrying Zipporah, the daughter of Jethro, Moses had almost put his past life behind him when God approached him on the holy mountain, Horeb.

To the astonished and terrified Moses, God gave instructions for releasing his people, Israel, from slavery in Egypt. Moses, after many protestations, followed the message God gave him and the result was an epic journey, famed for all time.

Moses was not the only person to receive a message from God in the mountains. Bible records show that mountains were one of God's favorite places for giving directions to humankind. No doubt, in these isolated places of grandeur, humans are more ready to listen; it is easier to delve into the center of our being in a mountain setting.

George Gorman, in *The Amazing Fact of Quaker Worship*, describes this center of our being as "that quiet place which is the vital core of man's being: the deep focus of his self-consciousness. It is from this center that all creative energy radiates, and to which men must constantly return for renewal in the necessary ebb and flow of life."

Gorman adds a comment about a decision he made at his center: "I am convinced that it was not only the best solution that I could find at the time, but also one that was absolutely right for me. Furthermore, in a strange sense it was ultimately given to me."

There are many recorded times when going apart, settling down, and waiting brings answers. I recall particularly reading about Norman Vincent Peale, when he was invited to minister in two churches. Which should he accept? It was after a night of prayer by both the Peales that they received definite guidance to go to the New York City church—which was then in an unpromising area. Going apart, centering down, earnestly waiting divine leading, had brought results.

William Stidger, too, went apart to hear God speak; his solitary place was not a city study but a mountain meadow.

> I heard God speak this day
> Along an Alpine way.
> 'Twas where a mountain shower
> Had washed a crimson flower
> Nodding in the blue heights
> When the rain was through.
> It bent as if in prayer
> Beneath the rain-washed air.
> 'Twas when the sun came out
> I thought I heard God shout
> With laughter down the seams
> And crevices and streams.
> I thought I saw His face
> In one high, holy place.
> —"I Heard God Speak"

John Muir, famed California author and environmentalist, also thought of mountains as message places: "Wherever we go in the mountains we find more than we seek."

I would like to paraphrase that: Wherever we go in the mountains, we find what we seek.

Our Father God, always more ready to give guidance and direction than we are to receive it, help us to understand that mountain vastnesses, both present and remembered, can aid us in finding your will for us and in charting life's course; in Jesus' name. Amen.

The Way

When you have brought forth the people out of Egypt, you shall serve God upon this mountain.
—Exodus 3:12*b* (RSV)

The Appalachian Trail is known as the longest continuously marked footpath in the world. It stretches 2,050 miles through 14 states, from Springer Mountain in Georgia to Mount Katahdin in Maine. This hiking path wanders through forests, twists around rocks, detours by large trees, climbs up mountains, and advances over wilderness meadows.

I have been on only small sections of this trail in the White Mountains of New Hampshire, but there are people (up to 4 million a year, according to the Appalachian Trail Conference) who hike at least a part of the trail each year, and many go the entire length.

Whether one hikes a little or a lot on this wilderness path, the spell of nature is there. The trail leads to a world forgotten, a place where man is permitted a rare glimpse of a vast natural world. This is the "forest primeval" of Henry Wadsworth Longfellow's *Evangeline*. Here the hiker feels like a small cog in a great natural cycle, rather than a master over the environment.

I recall the absolute silence—broken only occasionally by a bird call, the rustle of a small animal dashing into its burrow, or the tinkle of a stream as it dances downward on its way to the sea. The experience evoked an ethereal, otherworldly feeling, and I suddenly found that I was on a very special Way.

My thoughts reverted to the ancient story of Moses, who led the Israelites out of Egypt after decades of slavery. I find it significant that God instructed Moses to bring the Israelites to a mountain for worship after leading them to freedom. What a special Way that journey was for those Israelites!

This called to mind Christ's words, "I am the Way," and I realized that my Appalachian Trail experience, like that of the Israelites, was actually worship. When a silence "comes alive" in a prayer group, in a church service, or in individual meditation, the atmosphere is as hushed as on a mountain trail. As the worshiper settles into quiet, stills the mind, and centers on God, he or she enters new country, like the hiker of the present or the Israelite of old.

But often we are reminded of the frailty of the Way! On the Appalachian Trail a pile of rubbish and the distant hum of motors reminded me that in more settled areas, housing developments and increasing urban population threaten this sanctuary of nature. The trail is never far from villages and often is close to cities. Eternal vigilance is needed to protect it.

The inward Way is similarly threatened, I mused. The hectic pace of modern living and the constant barrage of noise pulls us away from the quiet so necessary to nourish our souls. I cringe when I see joggers or roller skaters with earphones clamped on their heads. I wonder why some young people feel the need for mechanical entertainment at every waking moment.

I resolve that part of each day will be spent in quiet—with no noise other than a bird's chirp or a squirrel's rustle. While my hands are busy clearing the table, making the bed, addressing a letter, or writing an article, my heart will be free to be on the Way.

The Quaker mystic Thomas Kelly expressed it more clearly in *Testament of Devotion:* "On one level we may be thinking, discussing, seeing, calculating, meeting all the demands of external affairs. But deep within, behind the scenes, at a profounder level, we may also be in prayer and adoration, song and worship and [have] a gentle receptiveness to divine breathings."

Our Father, originator of the Way, remind us when we stray that your path is a very special Way. Help us to follow the trail you have prepared for your followers from ancient times till today, that we may enter fully into the mountaintop experience you have designed for us; in Jesus' name. Amen.

Silence

You were on the holy mountain of God.
—Ezekiel 28:14*b* (RSV)

The older I grow, the more I appreciate silence. One place where perfect silence can be achieved is on a mountain, high above the timberline. Only the drone of an occasional plane breaks this place of perpetual quiet.

I remember sitting on an outcropping of rock some years ago after a steady upward climb of several hours. I relaxed in the natural arm chair, reveling in the peace and quiet, absorbed by the view. The world spread out below was diminished, microscopic. A church in the meadow seemed a child's toy; the red roofs surrounding it, miniature blocks. As I sat enthralled, my rapid pulse slowed. The world with its joys and woes never had seemed farther away. A peace, a oneness with creation, stole over me.

I recalled that experience recently when I read of a Quaker who had rushed from his home after a family quarrel. According to the account in *The Amazing Fact of Quaker Worship*,

once outside he walked at a fast pace towards a nearby hill, fuming vigorously over the righteousness of his cause and the crass stupidity of his family. The higher he climbed the more the surrounding countryside was disclosed to him. As this penetrated his consciousness he realized he was being calmed by it. Finally on the top of the hill he sat down to enjoy the sheer delight of his surroundings. Gradually a deep peace grew within him as he absorbed fully the loveliness of what he was seeing—how peaceful everything was. This aroused in him a strong sense of identity with the natural things around him, he felt part of the good earth.

Inevitably he compared his present state with the recent turmoil in his family below. . . . The quarrel was after all, but a superficial happening. He knew that the deep love and affection, which was the basis of this family life, continued unharmed by the explosion. Finally, he knew this truth deep inside himself, where he had discovered a quiet still centre which had become available to him when he was truly silent.

In my later years I have come to appreciate the silence of Quaker worship. The members of the Religious Society of Friends gather each Lord's day to worship in quietness.

Occasionally the silence is broken by someone who feels led to give a message, but the emphasis is on listening. They feel God's presence, knowing God not in theory but in fact.

Robert Barclay, writing in the seventeenth century, testified, "When I came into the silent assemblies of God's people, I felt a secret power among them which touched my heart; as I gave way unto it I found the evil in me weakening and the good raised up."

Both the silence of a mountain and the silence in worship produce a climate that allows me to reach that still center in my being where I am not alone but am connected with the Source of all light and love.

A busy physician once prescribed for himself a daily dose of silence every day after lunch. When asked what happened during that period, he replied, "I just sit still and clear my mind—get in tune with the Infinite. It relaxes me and brings me peace."

I am not always free to climb a mountain, and I cannot always slip away to a Quaker meeting, but like that busy doctor, I can determine again to set aside times of silent meditation. In my mind I will go to a mountaintop for guidance and strength—a place Ezekiel called the holy mountain of God.

Our Father, God of the high places and the low, help us to remember that it is necessary for our spiritual health to seek you in quietness. Nudge us to set aside the cares in our lives so that we may find direction and mount up with strength as the eagles; in Jesus' name. Amen.

The Two Faces of Clouds

Touch the mountains, that they smoke!
—Psalm 144:5b (RSV)

The two faces of clouds have always intrigued me. Some that sweep low, collecting around mountaintops and obscuring the view, are not at all welcome. Others, glowing with celestial colors at sunset, are a source of admiration.

I recall climbing Mount Washington some years ago on the first leg of a three-day excursion in the Presidential Range. That night we were to stay at the Appalachian Mountain Club's Lakes-of-the-Clouds hut. The long climb up the trail with packs on our backs was arduous, but we did not mind. We were already anticipating the glorious views of tomorrow's hike, when we would be following the much easier trail across the summits of Mounts Adams and Jefferson to Madison. I thrilled at the very thought.

To our dismay, we woke the next morning to a world of gray mist. Clouds had moved in during the night and covered the summits. Instead of the wonderfully clear day promised by the weatherman, we were faced with a long day in the fog.

With no prospect of expansive views, we scrapped our plans and descended the same trail we had climbed the previous day, rejoicing when we reached the cloud line and could see afar once more.

On the other hand, many years later, on a giant jet carrying me east from San Diego, I rejoiced to be among clouds. As we flew high over mountain ranges, the pilot guided the huge plane between puffs of white floating in a postcard-blue sky. Like giant mounds of whipped cream, the clouds glistened in the sunlight. I amused myself by finding faces and shapes among the white powder puffs. Certain mounds were uncannily like some mountaintops I had seen.

I have thought many times since about the two faces of clouds, or God's "smoke," as Isaiah called them, and I have found a parallel in human life. The cloud faces are not unlike the events that greet us in life. Some are happy, filled with sunshine, while others are gray and bring sadness.

One of the gray events descended on me at the sudden death of my beloved husband. My first reaction was a sense of loss and desolation. A numbness pervaded me and my heart refused to accept what my mind knew was so. Then gradually I came to know inwardly that this separation was only temporary. Pierre had gone on to another world where there was no sorrow and sighing. Someday I would join him there. Beyond the gray cloud line of today, the sunshine of tomorrow was waiting.

Also, though I did not welcome my gray cloud, I must admit that when it came it forced me into a deeper faith. God's smoke has two faces in the spiritual world, as it has in the natural.

Recently I came across a poem on this theme—"Friendly Obstacles," by an unknown author.

> For every hill I've had to climb,
>   For every stone that bruised my feet,
> For all the blood and sweat and grime,
>   For blinding storms and burning heat,
> My heart sings but a grateful song—
> These were the things that made me strong!
>
> For all the heartaches and the tears,
>   For all the anguish and the pain,
> For gloomy days and fruitless years,
>   And for the hopes that lived in vain,
> I do give thanks, for now I know
> These were the things that helped me grow!

'Tis not the softer things of life
  Which stimulate man's will to strive;
But bleak adversity and strife
  Do most to keep man's will alive.
O'er rose-strewn paths the weaklings creep,
But brave hearts dare to climb the steep.

Our loving Father who places us in this imperfect world, help us to realize that though problems come our way, good can result from them. When gray clouds hover over our days, guide us through them to a brighter outlook and to a deeper faith; in Jesus' name. Amen.

Beyond the Horizon

And in the Spirit he carried me away to a great, high mountain, and showed me the holy city Jerusalem coming down out of heaven from God.
—Revelation 21:10 (RSV)

A view of mountain peaks is inspiring from any angle, but when whole ranges are viewed from the top of a mountain the vista is positively awe-inspiring.

I recall enjoying such a view of the San Jacinto range after a scary trip by tram car up to the Mountain Station in Palm Springs, California. As the car swung back and forth on its almost vertical rise, my stomach flip-flopped. But I forgot the discomfort when I reached the top. To the east there was a flat sandy plain. But the view to the west revealed a breathtaking sea of mountains. Great waves of rock dipped and crested in folds to a limitless horizon in the distance.

The words of novelist Mary Waller in *The Wood Carver of 'Lumpus* came to mind. Her female protagonist, who was visiting in the Tyrol, "gazed on the mountain sea of Oetzthaler Alps, the white crests of its great rock waves caught in marvelous folds. . . . When morning comes it kindles its light from beacon to beacon while the whole serrated horizon flashes with rose and gold." She, like me, was impressed with the horizon—or rather the lack of it.

I have thought a great deal about horizons and the forever beyond which we cannot now see, since the passing from this world of my beloved husband. One morning he stepped from his car beside a busy highway after a minor accident. The next moment, his spirit had left his body for the world beyond the horizon. I knew when I saw his body-house later that the Pierre I had loved was not there. His spirit had preceded me to a place I did not yet know. Yet in a way I did know it, for through these many years I have sensed a presence, a caring love beyond reason or sight.

The novelist Adela Rogers St. Johns has felt that presence, too. In her recent book *No Good-byes: My Search for Life Beyond Death,* she tells how the loss of her son in World War II expanded her spiritual horizon. Through contacts from him in another world, and through others who have reported similar experiences, she has come to feel that those who have died have simply passed into another room. "There is life beyond death. . . . Death is not a closing but an opening of a door. . . . It is not the end of a relationship, just a change in relationship."

I believe this, for I have sensed similar intimations. In the weeks following Pierre's entrance into the next life, I pondered about its reality for me. Then early one morning while I was still only half awake, a subdued light outlined a cross on the "Christian" door of our bedroom. (This is a common type of colonial design, with a cross piece.) I had lived in that house for twenty years and never had that experience before. A few moments later, the light glowed again, then once more faded away.

    I have not see that light since, but I thought then, and I still do, that this was a confirmation of my belief that Pierre was alive and well beyond the horizon. It was a vision of the New Jerusalem mentioned by the apostle John. It was a beacon, flashing the good news from peak to peak, crossing the barrier of our limited horizon.

Our heavenly Father who anguishes with us when we grieve and sends comfort through the barrier of time, we praise you for your caring. Bless you for sending intimations of the world beyond the horizon. Guide us so to live that we may be worthy of entering the New Jerusalem when our call comes; in Jesus' name. Amen.

A Heavenly Voice

*We heard this voice borne from heaven,
for we were with him on the holy mountain.*
—II Peter 1:18 (RSV)

Rob Taylor, an avid mountaineer who overcame a childhood fear to become a professional Alpinist, recalls in *The Breach* his youthful puzzlement when a mountain drew him like a magnet on his first climbing expedition. By trail's end he had decided that "man is really comprised of two parts: a body which is material, set upon the earth, and a spirit, which is an invisible substance, a soul inside a body. Bound together they make up a man. Mountains are special places that spirits love, places they somehow can, for a short time, be released and free."

When Rob was older, he traveled the continents and climbed the summits of the earth's giants. In an unsuccessful attempt to climb "the breach," a massive solid ice waterfall on Africa's Mount Kilimanjaro, he had a near-fatal accident. As he lay for several days awaiting rescue, his earlier feeling was reinforced as his spirit seemed to reach out toward the invisible.

It is strange. God is so much in my thoughts these days. There is something special of Him here—on the flanks of this mountain. His presence hangs in the air like the smell of burning incense. I cannot smell it, but almost. I can almost touch it, taste it. It is a feeling whose origin lies beyond the usual boundaries of flesh and spirit. I feel as if I were immersed in His being.

There is no need for prayers. The lines of communication between God and me transcend words, perhaps even thoughts, reaching to the soul itself. While I am a solitary man upon this mountain, I am not alone. I am watched over, I am close to home. I sense it so strongly it is almost frightening.

Like Peter, Taylor had heard a heavenly voice on the mountain.

I used to think that these experiences come only to someone in great danger or extreme illness. I thought encounters like Taylor's were unique, rare happenings. But after reading *Christian Maturity* by E. Stanley Jones, I realized that these experiences are open to all of us. We do not need to be in dire circumstances to sense God's presence vividly.

Jones writes that we all have a divine discontent within us

which impels us to climb to a higher life. It is God's call to us to grow to spiritual maturity. He is beckoning to us. The devout mystics and the spiritually faithful affirm that God's presence is ready and available to all of us, if we but discipline ourselves to attend him.

And what kind of Father would God be if he did not disturb us toward maturity? No earthly parent would be content to have a child who refused to grow up. The parents' joy is in development, in growth, in going toward maturity. God cannot be otherwise and still be God, our Father. . . . He loves us too much to let us settle down into halfwayness.

Looking back on my life, I can point to experiences of God's closeness that came as the result of trauma, anxiety, and trouble. Ruefully, I cannot count as many times when these occurred during the sunny times of my life. It is clear that I have more work to do in the spiritual realm.

I take comfort in Jones' next words: "If God and life and we ourselves *will* maturity, then there is nothing on heaven or earth that can stop us from being the mature persons we ought to be. We are destined to be mature, and that destiny is written into every cell of our bodies."

Our Father who has planted in our genes the divine discontent that urges us to climb upward on the spiritual path, help us to will our own advance. Show us the restrictions that hold us back and the resources you have available, that we may grow more fully into maturity and into your presence; in Jesus' name. Amen.

A Book of Hours

*For, lo, he that formeth the mountains, and createth the wind,
and declareth unto man what is his thought,
that maketh the morning darkness,
and treadeth upon the high places of the earth,
The LORD, The God of hosts, is his name.*
—Amos 4:13

In the Middle Ages, monks developed a devotional pattern around the striking of the clock. The sound of the hourly bell called them to a time of prayer—a time of thinking about God. It is a discipline that has always intrigued me.

Jeremy Taylor, a seventeenth-century writer, explained it thus: "When the clock strikes, or however else you shall measure the day, it is good to say a short ejaculation every hour, that the parts and returns of devotion may be the measure of your time; and so do also in all branches of thy sleep, that those spaces which have in them no direct business of the world may be filled with religion."

In those days, each Book of Hours was individually written and beautifully illustrated for private devotions. I am happy to report that the printing press, modern communications, and a perceptive writer have brought the idea up to date. Novelist Elizabeth Yates has given us a modern *Book of Hours* which is of valuable assistance in our outreach toward God. She has compiled a meditation, accompanied by a verse and a prayer, for every hour of the twenty-four, beginning at 6:00 A.M., and notes that "the aim of any discipline of prayer is to become constantly aware of our relationship to God, not in panic or praise or sudden trial but at all times."

Prayer then gradually becomes a constant undergirding. "It is a holding, not only when the clock strikes but in all the moments in between, as one can still think of a friend while engaged in some activity; as a writer or artist will continue inwardly to develop an idea while outwardly carrying on a routine task."

She speaks of frets and anxieties, repeating the old saying, "When you get to your wit's end, you'll find God lives there." But she also follows the pattern of Amos, looking for God in the morning darkness and as the prime mover of nature. She finds him in a dense fog and on a hilltop in the sunrise.

I am truly grateful for devotional classics like this. I falter so often, or find myself too tired to keep a prayer schedule, that the striking of the hour can gently pull me back to my chosen path.

I wonder if Alfred, Lord Tennyson had this discipline of the hours in mind when he put these words into the mouth of King Arthur:

> More things are wrought by prayer
> Than this world dreams of. Wherefore, let thy voice
> Rise like a fountain for me night and day. . . .
> For so the whole round earth is every way
> Bound by gold chains about the feet of God.
> —*Morte D'Arthur*

Father of all, in all, around all, and above all, help us to remember you every moment of the day, but particularly at the striking of the hours. May we be part of the golden chain that connects all humans with you; in Jesus' name. Amen.

Receptivity

For the king of Israel has come out to seek my life, like one who hunts a partridge in the mountains.
—I Samuel 26:20b (RSV)

Nestled in the foothills of the Blue Ridge Mountains of North Carolina is Montreat, a year-round conference center of the General Assembly of the Presbyterian Church in the United States. I recall journeying there for a retreat, standing outside the inn and gazing over Lake Susan to the surrounding hills, agleam with autumn gold interspersed with scarlet. As I breathed in the invigorating pine-scented air and reveled in every nuance of the view, I rejoiced at this opportunity to draw apart and rest for awhile. I was looking forward to spiritual as well as physical refreshment.

The time for opening worship was drawing near and I turned to go inside, wondering about the term *retreat*. My first introduction to it some years ago had been negative. Should we not *advance* the cause of Christianity, rather than *retreat*? Historically, retreat means to *withdraw*. When applied to an army, this is negative, but I discovered that when it is applied spiritually, it is positive. For one's soul to be renewed, it is necessary to retreat. This is a call to "purify oneself, to regain a sense of communion with God," wrote John Oliver Nelson, former director of Kirkridge, another retreat center, in the heart of Pennsylvania's Pocono Mountains.

There is definitely an urge within us to seek God, and it is easier to do so when one leaves the everyday world. I remembered psychiatrist Viktor Frankl's statement that the God-urge is native to man and that 50 percent of Frankl's patients suffered from the suppression of this God-urge in their lives.

The words of Samuel in the Old Testament are as appropriate today, it seems. "For the King of Israel has come to seek my life, like one who hunts a partridge in the mountains."

But what should be our response to this divine call? It is not enough just to draw apart and enjoy the beautiful surroundings of nature. What should our attitude be? What should we do in these times of retreat?

The late missionary E. Stanley Jones comes to my rescue again as he so often does with his legacy of helpful books. In *Christian Maturity* he tells us,

> The first law of life is receptivity. . . . We can expend only what we receive and no more. . . . The nervous, pushing, active type of modern living has lost the art of receptivity, of being quiet, of listening. It pushes against the problems of living and exhausts itself upon these problems. Hence our mental institutions are filled with disrupted, exhausted persons.
>
> We are looking at the necessity of receptivity, of listening, of taking. . . . When expenditure is greater than intake, decay sets in. And if expenditure is kept up, then death results. Receptivity is a maturity *must*.

So that is why we long to draw apart, I reflected as the retreat leader began the call to worship. If we are to become mature spiritually, develop the talents God has planted within us, and increase our power of spiritual reproduction, we must be receptive to God's seeking. We must listen, rather than verbalize. Jones continues,

> In recent years I have found myself waking in the early morning hours. Instead of fretting about not being able to sleep, I decided I would turn that wakeful period into what I call my Listening Post. I say to the Father "Have you anything to say to me?" Then I relax and become perfectly passive and listen with all my being. For what he tells me may have life importance. Sometimes it is a small thing, "Write that letter!" Sometimes it is big, involving a real change in life and attitude. Sometimes he draws me into wordless communion with

Himself. Thus a possible fretful period has become a very fruitful period.

As if on cue, the retreat leader announced a time of corporate silence.

Dear God who loves us so dearly and pursues us so relentlessly, help us to quiet our minds and hearts in order to be receptive to your promptings. Remind us, when our strength is lessening, that we need to be open to your Spirit, that we may be invigorated and inspired to further your work; in Jesus' name. Amen.

Down from the Mountain

*And after six days Jesus took with him
Peter and James and John,
and led them up a high mountain apart by themselves;
and he was transfigured before them.*
—Mark 9:2 (RSV)

The disciples must have wondered why Jesus was leading them ever upward, as they toiled behind him on the mountain path. The Scripture tells us it was a high mountain—possibly Mount Tabor. In any event, it was far from the rest of humanity, a place set apart from the crowds.

Peter, James, and John followed, unquestioning, over the barren, rock-strewn trail so typical of the high places in the Holy Land. But they must have welcomed the rest stop. We can imagine their enjoyment of the panorama of green meadows and rolling hills as they relaxed in the warm sun. Perhaps they hardly noticed that Jesus had withdrawn from them and stood deep in prayer.

Soon, though, a strange light drew their gaze toward him. Astonished, they saw "the appearance of his countenance was altered and his raiment became dazzling white . . . and there appeared to them Elijah with Moses and they were talking with Jesus."

Afterward, overcome by this radiant encounter, the impetuous Peter proposed, "Let us make three booths, one for you, one for Moses, and one for Elijah." But Jesus led them back down the mountain, instructing them to tell no one what they had seen until he had been raised from the dead. There is a world in need, he gently inferred, and building a shrine on a mountaintop will not meet its problems.

How often this temptation returns. We wish to remain on the mountaintop, reveling in a place of retreat, hugging to ourselves the high spiritual experiences.

But like the disciples, we too are called to go down the mountain, away from its vastness and peace into the bustling world with its human needs. Our mountaintop periods of refreshment and inspiration are to be followed by times of work and service. The former provides the impetus and strength for the latter.

E. Story Hildreth reflects on this thought in "The Silent Places."

> I have come back from the mountains,
> And the beauty of forest ways,
> From the pine-trail winding at sunset
> To the crags in the purple haze.

I have come back from the prairies
And the free-born winds of the west.
There my soul reached out to heaven
And found in the starlight, rest.

I have come back to the city
With its clang, and its screeches and din;
Its halls are filled with madness
And its eyes are blind with sin.

I think of the peaks white-crested,
and the sage on the sweeping plain
And the vastness and the silence
And the whisper of God again.

Creator of mountains and of humankind, help us to hold close in our hearts the memory of mountain experiences. May we be able to recall the vastness and the silence, even though bound about by bustling days. May these majestic reminders of your presence renew us for the tasks ahead; in Jesus name. Amen.

He Depends on Us

*Now the eleven disciples went to Galilee,
to the mountain to which Jesus had directed them.
—Matthew 28:16 (RSV)*

Like so many events of Jesus' earthly life, one of the last took place on a mountain. When Jesus wished to bid farewell to his disciples, he directed them to climb a mountain.

The Scriptures report that Jesus appeared to his eleven

remaining disciples and charged them to "go ye therefore and teach all nations, baptizing them in the name of the Father and of the Son and of the Holy Ghost: teaching them to observe all things whatsoever I have commanded you."

I can picture that scene on the mountain's arid, rocky terrain. The disciples look apprehensively at one another as they receive the charge. Dismayed, they wonder how a handful of uneducated men could carry on this work. I can imagine their relief and joy at Jesus' final words: "Lo, I am with you always, even unto the end of the world."

I often muse on those long-ago moments and sense the mixture of joy and responsibility felt by the disciples as they walked back down the mountain trail. Theirs was a big job, but as long as Jesus would be with them, they knew they had a hope of succeeding.

That mixture of joy and responsibility is mine too, for I am part of today's generation which has inherited the charge. Jesus has depended on each succeeding generation to pick up the gospel and carry it forward. Sixty generations have been faithful since that long-ago day on the mountainside. I wonder about my own.

I am encouraged by a report given on the occasion of the 175th anniversary of the Haystack Prayer Meeting, when five students of Williams College in Massachusetts laid the groundwork for a worldwide missionary movement. "Today there are Christians in every nation on earth. There are well-established, self-governing churches, and they too are sending out young men and women into the world for mission."

I reflect that Jesus' charge was not given to an ecclesiastical organization, to a political party, or to an organized kingdom. That charge was given to eleven souls on a mountain. All they possessed was their time, talent, treasure, and will. In someone's fanciful tale, Jesus was asked what he would do if these men failed him. Jesus answered, "I have no other plan."

I feel a burden on my shoulders as I soberly recall that Christianity is always one generation from extinction. If we fail to win others to Christ, there will be no church in the future. Perhaps Calvin W. Laufer had this in mind when he wrote:

> O Master of the loving heart,
>   The Friend of all in need,
> We pray that we may be like Thee
>   In thought and word and deed.
>
> Thy days were full of kindly acts;
>   Thy speech was true and plain;
> And no one ever sought Thee, Lord,
>   Or came to Thee in vain.
>
> Thy hand was warm with sympathy;
>   Thy hand God's strength revealed;
> Who saw Thy face or felt Thy touch
>   Were comforted and healed.
>
> O grant us hearts like Thine, dear Lord;
>   So joyous, true, and free
> That all Thy children everywhere
>   Be drawn by us to Thee.
>   —"A Prayer Poem"

But I am comforted by the words of E. Stanley Jones: "You don't have to be a saint to share Jesus, but you do have to be sincere." I am further comforted when I realize that these words of Jesus were meant for me too: "Lo, I am with you always, even unto the end of the world."

Our Father, Lord of generations past and generations to come, help us to feel the responsibility that being a Christian brings. Enable us, with your help, to reach people within our radius with the good news of the gospel; in Jesus' name. Amen.